T0323794

FRAGMENTS:

ESSAYS IN SUBJECTIVITY,

INDIVIDUALITY AND AUTONOMY

Fragments:
Essays in Subjectivity, Individuality and Autonomy

Pedro Blas González

Algora Publishing
New York

ISBN: 0-87586-370-1 (softcover)
ISBN: 0-87586-371-X (hardcover)
ISBN: 0-87586-372-8 (ebook)

Library of Congress Cataloging-in-Publication Data —

González, Pedro Blas, 1964-
    Fragments: essays in subjectivity, individuality, and autonomy / by Pedro
Blas González.
        p. cm.
    Includes bibliographical references.
        ISBN 0-87586-370-1 (pbk: alk. paper) — ISBN 0-87586-371-X (alk.
paper) — ISBN 0-87586-372-8 (ebook)
        1. Literature—Philosophy. 2. Literature, Modern—20th century—
History and criticism. 3. Philosophy--Miscellanea. I. Title.

    PN49.G632 2005
    801—dc22

                                    2005000278

Printed in the United States

To Anne, Marcus Julian, and Isabella Sophia, for the light

TABLE OF CONTENTS

Table of Contents

PROLOGUE

DAWN

First there is the morning — primeval morning, the one of eternal consequence. The only discernible movement in this initial parting from form belongs to the dew, stretching down from the leaves. But the absence of sunlight makes this primary manifestation of being elusive. When does the separation of being from essence first take place? And when does the solidity of being become splintered with a vagrant multiplicity?

That first morning determined the tonic of time. In its first phase, the dethronement of understanding by reason castrated Cronos into oblivion. But this cosmic falling out was clouded in mist, giving subsequent observers the misguided impression of an early permanence. Thus, this was the last vestige of imagination. When the mist of this primordial morning cleared, the world already felt old and weary. To counter this early fatigue imagination needed to exercise a vital will.

To this day imagination demands of its practitioners a vital root in a conscious will. If most fail in this task — the answer, at best, is comically clear: the senses and the over-luminous brightness of midday have forever ensconced man in a failed material condition.

THE SECOND MORNING

The second day breaks with a heavy blanket of dew that covers the harshness of the land. In the distance...a figure walks gallantly toward the horizon. He holds the Sun high above his head. Flinging the giant sphere into the void of space, he settles down to admire his work — his tenacity. A smile now drips from his mouth, as he sits on the wet ground to praise his vision.

From the opposite horizon another figure quietly emerges from the young chaos of this emanation. Zeus grabs Prometheus by the back of the neck, as the younger man struggles to free himself. He scolds him: "Indiscretion is born of ill-reasoned thoughts — and quite often from a mere negation."

As a ghastly eagle feasts on Prometheus' liver, high on Mount Caucasus, his patience intensifies, grows. Anticipation now becomes ossified. Awaiting the next night that brings renewal, he views himself as irreverent — proud. The following day the eagle returns — Prometheus waits in guarded expectation — he flinches with the initial stab of pain until this, too, becomes part of the order of things.

"What," he muses, "can I do?" — what else, but continue to take his cue from his friend Sisyphus.

INTRODUCTION

> And if truth is one of the ultimate values, it seems strange that no one seems to know what it is. Philosophers still quarrel about its meaning and the upholders of rival doctrines say many sarcastic things of one another. In these circumstances the plain man must leave them to it and content himself with the plain man's truth. This is a very modest affair and merely asserts something about particular existents. It is a bare statement of the facts. If this is a value, one must admit that none is more neglected.
>
> — W. Somerset Maugham

In the first chapter of the second volume of *The Mystery of Being*, Gabriel Marcel convincingly argues that to philosophize is to think *sub specie aeterni*. Immediately thereafter he anticipates the question that some critics may pose: whether to reflect on the nature of the self is a form of ego-centrism. His answer is resoundingly clear. Marcel reasons that sooner or later the thinker has little choice but to realize that he is one of many entities. However, this initial discovery is founded on the understanding that the reality that we experience as a subjective-I is only one aspect of objective reality. Thus, we come to the realization that subjective reality — that is, human existence — is surrounded by a wider objective realm. Marcel's thought is illuminating, given his understanding that all reflection on the nature of the self must posit the fullness of life as a starting point. Abstractions inspire very little in terms of vital and existential existence. But to say that the self is surrounded by objective reality does not entail that it is readily absorbed by it. On the contrary, the subjective-I seeks to establish this demarcation point. The "bite of reality," as Marcel has referred to this outer reality, in effect has a disquieting and centralizing consequence that keeps the thinker humble. Ego centrism, whenever this occurs, then, only results from wearing blinders.

But let us now consider the question of why anyone would be concerned with the notion of subjectivity. After all, what advantage is there in giving oneself over to philosophizing on the nature of existence, to becoming burdened with the essence of being, given the extraordinary degree of distress that life naturally exhibits? Why does it seem so essential for thinkers — here, one must also include poets — to become bogged down with such weighty affairs? It is not necessary to open up a Pandora's box by addressing the complexity that "being" suggests, for it seems to me that the days of hair-splitting for the sport of it have not only failed to benefit man, but have served as a detriment to all vital philosophy. By being I merely mean the underlying substance of any existent — that is, of self-standing, self-subsisting reality. Such questions have been substantially addressed in the history of philosophy, by religion, and by science.

Why, then, this overarching concern for the nature of the self? Are the answers to such questions not categorically flexible enough to quench our existential inquietude? Ortega may have penetrated a fundamental truth of the human condition when he answered this very concern by suggesting that the value of this question has to do with human harmony. I will add that the reflective being is a harbinger, that is, an artisan of vital thought, of cohesion. But this unitary and cogent vital understanding that all existential reflection seeks is that of an inward glance. It is vital truth that man hopes for, while still obtaining to the dictate of naked reality. The best refutation of pure reason is often found in the cleavage that exists between the subjectively transcendent inner reality that defines man and reality as *physis* — as nature.

Naked reality, Ortega suggests, has us discover ourselves in the midst of a totality, of a confluence of things and people which always — and, this by definition, stand outside of what I am. Man seeks to know for the sheer necessity of knowing — the latter as a tool for living, as Ortega argues, "on what to rely on." Knowledge of any other kind simply falls into the category of the practical and expedient. Once again, I will reiterate that naked reality, as this is lived and felt from within, does not supply answers of any kind. The knowledge and answers that we seek, or at very best that we hope for, begin with a vital clarity of mind. To know what the extent of my vocation may be and to know that I may exercise this in some manner creates a harmony that levels the exigencies of naked experience to what is deemed manageable. Of course, this manner of reflection eschews all abstraction.

But if thought is an essential tool for a meaningful, well balanced, and contented existence, the question still remains as to what type of reflection is best suited for this vital task? One clear example of the type of thought that is not well suited for self-understanding is that whose preoccupation is with external objects or stimuli. Such thought cannot easily sustain itself while simultaneously negating the ground of a vital existent. Subjectivity, or what amounts to a conscious subject-will, cannot help but become confounded with inwardly reflexive questions. For this obvious reason we can say that science is quickly discarded as a suitable vehicle for self-understanding. Here, once again, if we need further convincing, we only need to look at objective contingencies. Human existence is not equivalent to human life. While human life can be explained in a quantifiable biologism, the former demands of

5

itself an existential account of time that can only be expressed through the recognition of autonomy.

The passage of time weaves out the value of thought and all that has been said, written, suggested, and forced upon man by motives that often fall short of the love of truth. I would argue that the history of the maxim as a viable, vital, and genuine form of human communication has the right intent, for instance. If one pays close attention to philosophers dating back to the pre-Socratics, the evidence seems to demonstrate an overwhelming and disproportionate attention to matters of man as a collective entity, the sphere of social-political organization, scientific concerns, the nature of thought, language and being. But everywhere we find a dearth of concentration on questions of what it is to be an individual. I suspect that some of the reasons for this collective and impersonal mania have to do with an incessant desire to find patterns in all things human. But I will also argue that this historical condition is partly due to the sheer boredom that some thinkers arrive at when dealing with matters of an autobiographical nature. There can be no doubt that temperament and vocation inform this task. Even further still, I would suggest that placing man in a collective container is easier, more economical and perhaps more expedient a solution to human concerns than to deal with personhood as a differentiated phenomenon: as self-conscious, individual entities. Unfortunately, most of these expedient solutions take on an undeniably political and hence public face. Such solutions become tainted with ideology at the service of power while shunning respect for truth and human autonomy. Yet another reason has to do with the psychological desire that most people have to belong to clans that promise to assuage the many blows of life itself. Understanding the fragile nature of human autonomy always comes at a profound personal price.

This latter point is particularly important given that man's steady stream of utopian (or dystopian) dreams seem best suited to the realm of the social-political, whereas individualists by their very nature are more concerned with the exigencies of existential reality.

These two realms do not have to be mutually exclusive by any means. But when we reflect on questions of temperament and personal autonomy we arrive at the realization that the essences that inform human existence are not easily quantified.

In Sumerian wisdom literature, the main character of the *Epic of Gilgamesh* (considered by many scholars to be the earliest example of wisdom literature) takes on the powers of life and death as he scours the world searching for immortality after his young friend Enkidu passes away. Not surprisingly, his incessant fight is taken to a court of appeals higher than anything his elders can advise him about. Gilgamesh is a microcosm of cosmic-subjective man. Albert Camus, too, embraces Gilgamesh's ethos in both *The Myth of Sisyphus* and *The Rebel*, where an inwardly vital intuition is stoically directed at life itself. Neither of his two major works vents their scorn (or pleads for mercy, as the case may be) to political powers or institutions, which in the final analysis always fail to provide a foundation for man's search for contentment, if not happiness.

Socrates, too, attempts to ground all knowledge in what is essential: self-knowledge or *auto-gnosis*. After having entertained the concerns of earlier thinkers, he proceeds to turn his attention to the conviction that a more pressing problem for man has to do with questions of self-understanding. The pre-Socratics concentrated on questions that took their overall cue from the natural elements. Socrates, noticing that this might turn out to be an existential cul-de-sac, reacted by demonstrating that the highest value was rational life and that this was best manifested in the moral life of man. Thus Socrates' dual quips, "Know thyself" and "The unexamined life is not worth living," would prove to be more than the fancy of someone overwrought with subjectivism. His was a practical ethical humanism that was based on the autonomy of the individual.

What can life viewed from within offer man in a technological age? This question seems especially pertinent to an age when human problems are confused with those of the natural sciences. Today, a segment of the human sciences continues to negate its viability as a mediator of existential essence by relentlessly imitating the method of science. Unfortunately, another considerable portion negates the reality of human essence altogether.

It has still not dawned on positivist thinkers that the methods of science and those of the humanities are not mutually agreeable. Technical problems are closed-ended in scope, that is, they are solvable, whereas existential questions are open-ended and are to be re-discovered by everyone on their own terms. No amount or degree of fashionable "theory" can succeed in negating reality. It is for this reason that technical questions are often easier to address and correct than human questions. Today, what man demands of science is not so much truth but an ever-expanding realm of technology. Thus every human life — human existence, when viewed from the inside out — is a fragment of reality, but a central fragment nonetheless. These are the conditions that life sets for us. Today, perhaps the possibilities for philosophy have never been greater and more fruitful — and yet more tragically squandered. For philosophy to become relevant once again, as the *grande dame* of humanism that she once was, it must strive to offer insight into questions of vital concerns for individuals, and not as a forceful, intellectual refutation of reality. The days of pointless analytical hair-splitting, self-referential word play, ideological canvassing, and self-consuming abrogation have proven to be an embarrassment to all thoughtful people. The nobility of the philosophical vocation is best appreciated when it is viewed as a tool in the service of life. What is at stake, then, is nothing less than the soul of man, not as an empty caricature set up by "theory" and its creators, but as a vital possibility. Unfortunately, today the humanities resemble a man who has been waiting for hours at a station for his train to arrive — when all of a sudden it dawns on him that the kind of train that he awaits can as easily be taken from the nearest drugstore, lecture hall or his living room.

In light of the work that has already been done in this area, a new approach seems justified — one that limits the degree of pedantry and which embraces a vital, real world reconstitution of the human condition. The following essays explore examples of the variegated forms that human autonomy and subjectivity can take, as these pertain to actual human beings. As the title of this work suggests, I am merely addressing aspects of the fragmented nature of the human condition. Hence the only pretension that this work makes is to treat human existential vitality as if it actually mattered. Individuals steeped in this process make no greater claims than to salvage their own temporal existence. What binds thinkers to this vital task has less to do with abstraction and post-modernist theory, as the latter is construed today, and more with flesh and blood, time-keeping, real world subjects.

CHAPTER 1. THE PLIGHT OF SUBJECTIVITY IN AN OBJECTIVE WORLD: EXISTENTIAL SUBJECTS IN SINISTER SITUATIONS

> To read is to make a transfusion of time. The hero lives on our life, our ignorance of the future. The dangers surrounding him are our own; with our reader's patience, he constructs a parasitic duration whose strand we break and resume at the pleasure of our moods. — Jean-Paul Sartre

The tension between appearance and reality is a central and perpetual theme in the work of Eric Ambler. Of all the subsequent themes found in his work, I will argue that none is as strong as the urge to intellectualize at the expense of reality itself. Ambler brings to the detective novel an ingenious literary/philosophical appeal that lifts this genre from its stale pre-World War I action-reaction operative mode. The intellectualizing and controlling of reality aspect in Ambler's work does battle with the open-ended superstructure that is human reality. The writer as amateur spy nonchalantly attempts to control reality, whereas reality proper, Ambler suggests, cannot be tamed. In effect, reality, or what presents itself as the world-at-large, operates more like the logic exhibited in the inductive method, with its seemingly endless realm of possibilities and eventual narrowing down to probability. Thus possibilities and chance in the objective world only give us probability and not the results found in the neatly cropped classical deductive logical method that the writer makes use of when writing fiction.

Ambler in effect realizes this early on in his career and seeks to develop these themes with conviction and deliverance. Hence, in this chapter my main objective is twofold: 1) to explore the relationship between logic, especially the deductive method, and the overall structure of literary notions of chance; and 2) how best to appropriate literary conventions in terms of human reality?

Eric Ambler begins *A Coffin for Dimitrios* with a description of the dual effect that chance and possibility play in the lives of ordinary people. He explains:

> It is one of those convenient, question-begging aphorisms coined to discredit the unpleasant truth that chance plays an important, if not predominant, part in human affairs. [1]

This disclaimer, which appears in the second paragraph of the book, has the narrator exclaim that a certain wise Frenchman named Chamfort has substituted providence for chance. The Chamfort that Ambler has in mind is Sebastien-Roch Nicolas Chamfort (1741-1794). Chamfort was a writer of maxims and a member of the Jacobins at the outbreak of the French Revolution. The aforementioned quote is a significant statement because it has the effect of leveling the seemingly logo-centric order of things into the intractable intricacies and antinomies found in reality. Chance, then, Ambler is quick to suggest, always informs human existence in

---

1. Eric Ambler. *A Coffin for Dimitrios.* Cleveland, Ohio: The World Publishing Company, 1939. p. 2.

the form of blind probability. But the writer-spies in his novels are always the last to find this out.

It is not an insignificant fact that this work was first published in England under the title *The Mask of Dimitrios* in 1939. The mask theme only serves as a figurative statement that attempts to cover up the illusive persona of the protagonist. Of course, nowhere in the novel does Dimitrios, a pre-World War underworld criminal, wear a mask. His identity, nevertheless, becomes a faceless persona that is shrouded in mystery. The mask, then, serves as a metaphor for the overall moral confusion of modernity. We can also argue that the mask motif can serve as a labyrinthine "who's who" amongst people in the murky criminal underworld.

While it is true that many people have heard of Dimitrios, few have ever seen him due to his many aliases and his care for concealment. But this seeming lack of being rooted in the affairs of a "genuine" existence is precisely what draws Latimer, the writer of intrigue novels, into the hunt for this specter of a man. But where is the Ariadne's thread that connects Dimitrios to the real world? Where can Latimer begin his search for this shady subject? And what role does chance play in the intermingling of these two distinct lives?

No doubt at first glance some critics might object to Ambler's treatment of logic. A possible reason for this is due to his supplanting of deductive reason with the inductive method or, what is worse, with raw chance. This may be the case, but Ambler nevertheless always has his protagonists reacting rationally to the haphazard demands of chance. Ambler's heroes always arrive at a point when they realize that they are in over their heads. However, they never lose perspective. What they do lose is a vital notion of the degrees of reality. In other words, these protagonists have a protracted sense of just how deep into an ominous reality they have entered. Thus, proactive reason is never totally sublimated. It is instead framed by the interplay that dominates a reasoned account of reality and the often-unwarranted direction that human existence must adjust to. Ambler goes on to add, "Inevitably, chance does occasionally operate with a sort of fumbling coherence readily mistakable for the working of a self-conscious providence."[1]

Admittedly, a voluntary giving up of one's reason to mere chance is neither a popular nor a safe way to uphold such a conviction. Such a notion of chance takes away our primal freedom as conscious agents of our own devices. Ambler, realizing this, merely calls this "an unpleasant truth." But this statement of truth as such cannot readily be understood in its immediacy. There is a dialectical, even a time-lapse, quality to the understanding that the aforementioned notion of chance mercilessly requires the passage of time to bear its fruit. Thus the inner constitution of chance is never readily seen in its immediacy, only its effects. Chance always plays the role of the spoiler in Ambler's work. Ambler pays close attention to this aspect of reality and thus develops his situations, themes, and characters accordingly. But what is meant here by the passage of time is not merely the common sense chronological ordering of reality that humans often take for granted. His readers are treated to the dialectical exigencies of a form of consciousness that seeks resolution to the antinomies that reality creates. However, Ambler does not state (let us be clear on this point) that the importance of reason in human existence ought to be downplayed. He merely subjugates our belief in providence to that of chance. Relegating the security and comfort found in providence to that of blind chance is merely a statement about the overall conditions of human existence. Thus, there is no explicit disregard for a reasoned account of reality in Ambler's work, any more than a pigeon walking on a window ledge displays an explicit disregard for the circumstances. Accidents, however, do occur. Yet accidents only happen to rational beings; and this by definition, Ambler seems to argue. Therefore, man, who is an existentially-driven being, must contend with an external world that is not of his choosing. This, then, is Ambler's main point of contention.

---

1. Ibid., p. 3.

Such notable historians of ideas as Polybius, Jacob Burckhardt and the twentieth-century Spanish philosopher José Ortega y Gasset have all proposed a vision of human life as an open-ended drama or narrative that is played out by each individual respectively. This notion that life viewed from within is the real essence of history is the crux of Ambler's statement on life and literature. He writes, "The fact that a man like Latimer should so much as learn of the existence of a man like Dimitrios is alone grotesque."[1] The vulgarity that Ambler has in mind has everything to do with the unexpected interaction of the world of these two individuals. What Ambler suggests is that perhaps in a utopia the worlds of these diametrically opposed people would never cross. Here, again, we find an early precursor to the themes that Ambler is to develop in the disinterested voice of the narrator throughout *A Coffin for Dimitrios*. Of course, this statement is rife with the understanding that modernity has leveled the world to such a degree that the life of a university professor/writer like Latimer can come into direct contact with a cold-blooded criminal such as Dimitrios. This is a telling statement, if not an all-out indictment of modernity in at least two respects: First, that the post-World War I social-political order has shrunk the world, both politically as well as culturally, and secondly that this new *Weltanschauung* now necessarily governs the rules and mores of engagement in such a world. Latimer suffers from the pulling-in effect, let us call it, which these new social conditions play on the innocent and unsuspecting. To be pulled in by circumstances that are not of our own design is precisely where our loss of control occurs.

Latimer first hears of this criminal, Dimitrios, from a Colonel Haki, who is head of the Turkish secret police. He meets Haki while attending a four-day party hosted by a Madame Chavez, a Turkish national who was formerly married to an Argentine meat broker. The two men begin to exchange thoughts on literature and the dominant conventions of the detective novel. Colonel Haki tells

---

1. Ibid., p. 4.

Latimer that he has written a novel titled, *The Clue of the Blood-Stained Will*. The Colonel asks Latimer to give him an honest evaluation of the work, which Latimer reluctantly does in the Colonel's office, not too far away, some time later. The Colonel's novel consists of a clichéd and tame murder that takes place in an English country house involving a will. This exchange bores Latimer, who is always meeting people who have also "written novels" that they want to share with him once they have learned that he is a writer.

But this apparently banal experience is to serve as an anticlimax to a much more sinister real world denouement to follow. This chance meeting between the writer and the police chief may seem romantic from the perspective of the writer, but it is very indicative of just how such entanglements get started. This introductory chapter ends with the Colonel asking Latimer if he would be interested in a real murder.

Chapter two begins with the narrator describing the shock that Latimer; a writer of fiction, receives when he is asked to contemplate the facts concerning a real murder case. This is the very first instance where the theme of real life versus literature first surfaces. The inversion from Latimer the writer of fiction and the Colonel as the aspiring writer to Latimer the real world crime novice and the Colonel as the tough secret police chief launches the novel to its next level. Colonel Haki and Latimer are discussing Dimitrios' life of violence and how a life of violence can lead to a violent death when Latimer exclaims, "At least he died by violence. That is something very like justice."[1] The Colonel interjects, "Ah! There is the writer speaking. Everything must be tidy, artistic, like a *roman policier*."[2] At this point the Colonel proceeds to give Latimer a detailed description of the delinquent, Dimitrios. This description is designed as a primer to root Latimer on firm, realistic soil as to the nature of true crime. After the Colonel has shown Latimer Dimitrios' police dossier, Latimer becomes interested. He becomes

---

1. Ibid., p. 19.
2. Ibid., p. 19.

so enmeshed in the life of this criminal, Dimitrios, that he requests to be shown his corpse.

Latimer's interest is not with crime or political intrigue, but rather with the worldview of this individual. Ambler is a keen observer of the metaphysical essences that inform the life of people. What Latimer becomes intent on knowing is the life trajectory of the criminal and how he viewed the world. This concern for Dimitrios' existential make up is important because one of the themes of the work has to do with the mere chance that these two different lives should cross each other at all. A particularly powerful scene occurs at the morgue when Latimer sees the body of the man whom he has now heard so much about. The ancient theme of appearance and reality comes into play in this scene once again. Latimer seems shocked to see the reality of a corpse, while the Colonel remains nonchalantly matter of fact. At this point Latimer is still intrigued by Dimitrios as a fictional entity, not as a spatial-temporal being. But in the morgue scene, these two perspectives collide. Latimer stares at the corpse in astonishment as he ponders, "So this was Dimitrios. This was the man who..."[1]

At this point the Colonel proceeds to explain to Latimer the internal workings of real-world intrigue, murder, and political assassination. These occurrences, he tells Latimer, are never tidy or logical. Instead, he tells him:

> I find the murderer in a *roman policier* [detective novel] much more sympathetic than a real murder. In a *roman policier* there is a corpse, a number of suspects, a detective and a gallows. That is artistic. The real murderer is not artistic.[2]

What he means is that in real-world situations there is no control on behalf of an observer. The Colonel seems to suggest that events that take place in real time are never as dramatic as when they are fictionalized. The immediacy of human reality often does

---

1. Ibid., p. 28.
2. Ibid., p. 17.

17

not allow for the luxury of a complete understanding of its terms. This assertion squarely counters the logical demands placed on the writer by the craft of writing. For this very same reason, a great number of detective works never bother to develop the fine details of a post-arrest scenario. Most readers are merely interested in the suspense and drama that they feel they help to unravel. Colonel Haki, then, is the first to counter Latimer's notion of the logically closed-ended deductive method with that of induction. The problem is that inductive proofs are never as elegant or sure-footed as deductive ones. In the deductive method the premises follow a prescribed order whose only demand is that the form be correct in achieving a valid conclusion. A classic example of this approach is exemplified by the following syllogism:

Premise: All men are mortal.

Premise: Socrates is a man.

Conclusion: Therefore, Socrates is mortal.

This syllogism is very much in keeping with Latimer's control over his fictional works.

Of course, this example of a categorical syllogism is formal in structure and validates what Haki tells Latimer about fictional murder being tidy and artistic. Here, the syllogism begins with the universal and categorical statement, "All men." This proceeds in the form of an inverted pyramid, and culminates in a particular closed conclusion that, given its valid form, cannot be otherwise but true. But Ambler supplants this reasoning with an inductive one that begins with particular premises and ends in a universal conclusion. Of course, this inductive scenario only serves to point out a condition of mere probability. Untidiness is the main characteristic of inductive reasoning.

At this point in the work Latimer begins to wonder who Dimitrios truly was. He becomes interested in uncovering the vital historicity of this criminal. The speculative questions that he poses, such as, "what makes a life?" and "what is a man?" are philosophical concerns that Colonel Haki never entertains. These questions are of an existential nature. Questions about the metaphysical "why?" of events, causes, etc. seem out of place in the presence of world-weary men like the Colonel. Haki, on the other hand, is much more interested in the more scientifically-oriented procedural question that merely has to do with the "how?" of things. However, in an unguarded reflective moment Haki does manage to say, "Life is very strange..."[1] At this stage in the novel's development, Latimer decides to go on a literary search to construct the existential life of Dimitrios Makropoulos by retracing his steps. But Latimer's project appears doomed to failure from the outset. He enlists the help of a willing translator, a Mr. Muishkin, another man of letters. Latimer's initial mistake is that he fails to realize that the kind of logic that is found in vital life, as Andre Breton argues in his masterful work of 1924, *Manifestoes of Surrealism*, is always more akin to chance than it is to formal validity. Breton writes:

> We are still living under the reign of logic: this, of course, is what I have been driving at. But in this day and age logical methods are applicable only to solving problems of secondary interest. The absolute rationalism that is still in vogue allows us to consider only facts relating directly to our experience. Logical ends, on the contrary, escape us. It is pointless to add that experience itself has found itself increasingly circumscribed.[2]

The logic of chapter four is an essential ingredient of the story because there we find Latimer excited about his search, a search that he intends to make purely literary in scope. During this moment in the book, Ambler has the narrator explain what is at stake in Latimer's ideals and actions. Ambler explores the many dichotomies of thought and implies that an overarching fact of the objective world is that action, regardless of being grounded in any a priori thought, is always governed by a self-guiding principle. Ambler's six great novels were written between 1936 and 1940,

---

1. Ibid., p. 30.
2. Ibid., 10.

years when the totalitarian impulse was at its height in Europe, either in actuality or in intent. This new world order of having to pay total allegiance to the state underscored the value of individual autonomy. This totalitarian impulse was by no means an illusory literary condition. Ambler and other writers and thinkers recognized this new reality as capable of becoming more the rule in Europe than the exception. It is for this reason that Ambler suggests that in such times we entrust ourselves to a blind faith that in some instances can destroy our ideals or... worse. He explains:

> The situation in which a person, imagining fondly that he is in charge of his own destiny, is, in fact, the sport of circumstances beyond his control is always fascinating. It is the essential element in most good theatre from the Oedipus of Sophocles to East Lynne. When, however, that person is oneself and one is examining the situation in retrospect, the fascination becomes a trifle morbid. Thus, when Latimer used afterwards to look back upon those two days in Smyrna, it was not so much his ignorance of the part he was playing but the bliss which accompanied the ignorance that so appalled him.[1]

The philosophical implications of Ambler's work are enlightening, I will reiterate, for at lease two reasons: first, we must consider that philosophical concerns are often most effective when entertained in non-explicitly philosophical discourse and vital situations, and not necessarily through what are often merely ostentatious and abstruse texts. Secondly, and more importantly, what makes a situation or concern philosophical does not owe its profundity to a particular theory, genre or form of writing, but is rather informed by the pathos exhibited by the questions or dilemmas at hand. This recognition is aptly manifested throughout Ambler's work.

The writer, Ambler suggests, has immense control over his work as he constructs situations that, while authentic in degree, nevertheless always remain at the level of fiction. The theme of

---

1. Ibid., p. 52.

writers and often, too, professors as agents or detectives of some kind or other is, in fact, very common. Amongst these we can mention a few, such as: Austin Freeman's character, *Dr. Thorndyke*; Jacques Futrelle's *Professor Augustus Van Dusen*; and Edmund Crispin's eccentric don, *Gervase Fen*, Oxford Professor of English Language and Literature. But probably one of the better examples of an actual major writer who has undertaken such an activity is that of Somerset Maugham's 1928 novel *Ashenden*, a work that is actually based on his own activities during World War I in Russia and Switzerland.

Maugham explains in the introduction to *Ashenden* that the work is "founded on my experiences in the intelligence department during the last war [World War I], but rearranged for the purposes of fiction." "Fact" he goes on to say, "is a poor storyteller."[1] His argument is that life should only serve as the raw material for literature. Maugham has stated that he is not interested in recreating life in fiction.

The science fiction writer Frederik Pohl shares the same conviction. The latter writes in, *The Way the Future Was*:

> Reality is a terrible annoyance to a novelist. It does not come in tidy packages. What I want to do is to shape the events of my life to fit a dramatic pattern.[2]

The question of chance versus providence is played out very diligently in Ambler's work. Because Latimer is nothing other than an ordinary man who is faced with extraordinary circumstances, he finds himself lost in a rather surreal maze of seemingly endless deception. This maze of ever-new circumstances leads him to depart from his normal life as he is launched into a maelstrom, with the reader's full empathy. It is not inconceivable that any one of us might come to find himself in such an imbroglio. This is the convention that the reader must accept from the outset of the novel. Perhaps the most human of factors in Latimer's character is his

---

1. Somerset Maugham. *Ashenden: The British Agent*. New York: Avon Books, 1951. p. 5.
2. Frederik Pohl. *The Way the Future Was*. London: Victor Gollancz, 1979. p. 252.

propensity for adventure and curiosity. One can take a philosophical position in this aspect of Ambler's work by suggesting that Latimer is attempting to unify all of his experiences into some cohesive center. Even though it is true that he has no immediate, that is, no actual experience of Dimitrios and the latter's world, he does have some knowledge, if only through hearsay, of such a world. — But one hears about all sorts of things, people, and events that we do not have to embrace, some critics will observe. This, of course, is true. However, this particular aspect of reality is congenial to Latimer's line of work as a writer. This is also akin to Max Scheler's hierarchy of values where we naturally gravitate toward values, that is, choices, that are in keeping with our overall core vision.

The theme of the unsuspecting writer appears in several of Ambler's books. In *The Dark Frontier*, his first book, written in 1936, the professor is Henry Barstow, a physicist. In *Background to Danger* (1937), the innocent intruder is Kenton, "an intelligent-looking journalist."[1] *The Schirmer Inheritance* (1953) features a Philadelphia corporate lawyer, George Carey, who goes to the Old World to settle an estate. However, the most interesting angle that Ambler offers the reader in *A Coffin for Dimitrios* is that of a writer who intellectualizes reality perhaps to the point of his own detriment.

When Latimer first embarks on the search for Dimitrios, his is simply a literary quest. Ronald J. Ambrosetti, writing in a "Twayne's English Authors" series titled *Eric Ambler* refers to Charles Latimer as the embodiment of the Nietzschean Apollonian ideal, while "Dimitrios is the Dionysiac avatar of a new age."[2] This notwithstanding, Latimer is attempting to discover the meaning, if any, of the kind of life that men like Dimitrios lead. Through this search Latimer not only learns the reality that Dimitrios' world entails, but also something about himself in the process.

What I find most enthralling about Latimer's descent and exploration into the underworld of crime and ruthless intrigue is

---

1. Eric Ambler. *Background to Danger*. New York: Bantam Books, 1968. p. 9.
2. Ronald J. Ambrosetti. *Eric Ambler*. New York: Twayne Publishers, 1994. p. 52.

the relationship that is forged between reason and crass immorality. Articulated in perhaps different terms, this relationship can be said to be that of a philosophical subjective journey undertaken by someone who has not delved too deeply into the queasy aspects of human life and the blind dictates of chance. Yet this is precisely what Ambler posits: the more Latimer views himself as being in control, the more ruthless and deceptive that his fate seems. Upon his arrival in Sophia, Latimer confides to Marukakis:

> As you know, I write detective stories. I told myself that if, for once, I tried doing some detecting myself instead of merely writing about other people doing it, I might get some interesting results. [1]

This admission has Latimer dropping pen and paper for a kind of logic that is based on actual tips and connections with those who have known Dimitrios personally. However, this is also a more concrete acceptance of a strange world that he has never witnessed firsthand. His initial concern with Dimitrios, he intimates, is manifested with a naïve sense of awe. Latimer reflects:

> My idea was to try to fill in some of the gaps in the dossier. But that was only an excuse. I did not care to admit to myself then that my interest was nothing to do with detection. It is difficult to explain but I see now that my curiosity about Dimitrios was that of the biographer rather than of the detective. There was an emotional element in it, too. I wanted to explain Dimitrios, to account for him, to understand his mind, I saw him not as a corpse in a mortuary but as a man, not as an isolate, a phenomenon, but as a unit in a disintegrating social system. [2]

The essential point to consider, Ambler seems to be suggesting, is that the literary implications that Latimer brings to this entire ordeal is, at first glance, a simple luxury. This rational convenience is afforded to Latimer — but not to Colonel Haki, given the

---

1. *A Coffin for Dimitrios*, p. 76.
2. Ibid., p. 77.

exigencies of real-world crime investigation. The scope of theory according to Haki must be kept to a discrete level that is mandated by the particulars of the actual case at hand. A failure to understand this is reminiscent of Kant's contention that transcendental knowledge comes as a result of our immanent awareness of our own thought. This reflection must, however, first come to terms with the chaos of sensations that is the transcendent or what amounts to the physical world. In other words, reality itself often dictates to us through reason what prudent course of action to embark on. Thus regarding this apparent failure, Ambler, through the passive voice of his narrative, offers the following forewarning:

> He had gone into the business believing his eyes to be wide open, whereas, actually, they had been tightly shut. That, no doubt, could not have been helped. The galling part was that he had failed for so long to perceive the fact. Of course, he did himself less than justice; but his self-esteem had been punctured; he had been transferred without his knowledge from the role of sophisti-cated, impersonal weight of facts to that of active participator in a melodrama.[1]

Latimer is quite serious about finding out something about Dimitrios that the police do not already know. However, it cannot be argued that he is playing a game. If Ambler took that line of thinking then his entire notion of chance would collapse. Instead, it is because Latimer has no apparent clue as to the danger that lies ahead that Ambler can build a case for the scholar/detective who stumbles into reality through mere chance. Latimer's interest is primarily psychological and reductionist in that he wants to know if he can uncover something substantially revealing about Dimitrios' past that is definitive of his embracing a life of crime. But this is risky business precisely because there are no biographies to read on Dimitrios. To be successful, Latimer must do the legwork himself, which means no less than talking to the people who knew Dimitrios. Amongst these people there are some who have been severely wronged by Dimitrios and thus enjoy spewing out all they

---

1. Ibid., p. 52.

know about the criminal. But others, like Madame Preveza, an independent-minded woman who owns a club that Dimitrios frequented, is very hesitant to talk about him. She tells Latimer that Dimitrios had some good points. This situation is a fine example of the naiveté of Latimer the writer vis-à-vis real world intrigue, as is showcased in Chapter Six, when Latimer and his translator, Mr. Marukakis, seem like two small children in the overpowering presence of the streetwise Madame Preveza. She is, like Dimitrios and all the other patrons of her club, "La Vierge St. Marie," an underworld figure who has very little patience or empathy for people of the likes of Latimer. She tells Latimer that she has read some detective novels and that she finds them ugly. She prefers love stories. She goes on to tell the two men:

> You do not need to know human nature for that. It is for love stories and romances that one must know human nature. Romans policiers are ugly."[1]

The clear implication is that she does not read about the world that she lives in. This theme of appearance and reality is fundamental to this literary genre. There is always an interesting paradox at play here in that Ambler argues that, because of the nature of the game, those who live out the life of crime cannot readily write or reflect on it. Yet the outsider never has a penetrating ability to see the inner workings of such a world, regardless of any theorizing.

As if the decision to seek out the true life of Dimitrios was not already challenge enough, Latimer runs into a further problem when a strange, heavy-set man appears in his hotel room. The man is there for the sole reason of asking Latimer what he knows of Dimitrios. Thus this is the level of intrigue that sees the start of Chapter Seven. Here, the second half of the novel begins. When the strange man, Mr. Peters, tells Latimer that this Dimitrios in whom Latimer has

---

1. Ibid., p. 101.

become so interested owes him money, Latimer becomes confused. Latimer had come to regard the dead Dimitrios as his own.

> He had come to regard Dimitrios as his own property, a problem as academic as that of the authorship of an anonymous sixteenth century lyric. And now, here was the odious Mr. Peters, with his shabby god and his smiles and his Luger pistol, claiming acquaintance with the problem as though he, Latimer, were the interloper.[1]

Mr. Peters wants to test Latimer's knowledge of Dimitrios' past, but also what he knows of his recent doings. In fact, Mr. Peters is testing Latimer's knowledge in order to inform Latimer that Dimitrios is very much alive. This development once more rattles Latimer's grasp of reality. As the novel progresses we see Latimer losing his grip on what he hitherto had considered to be real. This new realization also allows for the narrator to continue developing the notion of chance that was introduced at the start of the novel. Latimer's a priori notions of human nature do not stand up to the fortuitous ranting of *a posteriori* reality. Perhaps thinking of this problematic in pure Kantian terms can offer us a vision of what Latimer's true concerns are. Latimer's subjective and a priori preoccupation with "I think" has to be accompanied, as Stephen Korner writes in his excellent work, austerely titled *Kant*, "by all of my presentations."[2] The "I think" is what Kant calls the pure ego or the self attempting to make sense, that is, to unify all of its experiences. However, this pure ego cannot exist encapsulated within itself. At any given moment the pure ego, the "I think" which thinks abstractly, must manifest itself in the world, but now it must do so as an empirical ego or as a subject that must deal with its spatial surroundings.

When Latimer is first presented with the case of Dimitrios in Haki's office, he cannot help but view the situation with the a priori

---

1. Ibid., p. 109.
2. Stephen Korner. *Kant*. p.112.

apparatus of the detective writer. Haki, on the other hand, attacks Dimitrios' dossier like any other criminal case, by looking for patterns embedded in the particulars. The differences in method are striking. While Latimer's presuppositions concerning real world detection follow from his literary/philosophical method, Haki's remain that of a professional investigator. These two methods, of course, do not have to be mutually exclusive. The apparent difference is that while aspects of real world crime are used in literary detection, the same cannot be said to hold true of literary methods that attempt to cross over into real world detection. Instead, what Latimer encounters is a dialectical process that, even though composed of a number of stages, is not a complete process. Thus Latimer cannot apply to his means of detection what Kant refers to as "the fundamental principle of dialectical reason" because to do so would necessarily invoke a finished set of stages of the dialectic.[1] This is what I referred to previously as being a closed-ended deductive process. At best, Latimer can only employ inductive reasoning, which only has probability as its conclusion. Dialectical reason is Latimer's main tool of organization, which allows him to synthesize the different stages of the case as these become manifest.

This, of course, does not mean that such a method is totally fruitless within a literary framework. It merely means that the desired results cannot be achieved a priori. This realization becomes apparent to Latimer as the novel progresses. Hence, he begins to make adjustments to his "experiment" in deduction. One day he begins to reflect on his prospects for further trouble, when he decides to formulate a possible solution to the dilemma in which he now finds himself. Ambler explains:

> He had a choice of two courses of action. He could go back to Athens, work on his new book and put Dimitrios and Marukakis and Mr. Peters and this Grodek out of his mind. Or, he could go to

---

1. Ibid. p. 123.

Geneva, see Grodek (if there were such a person) and postpone making any decision about Mr. Peter's proposals.[1]

This realization halfway through the novel is an admission that things have gone too far. At this point Latimer becomes aware that he is no longer in control of the situation. He adds:

> The first course was obviously the sensible one. After all, the justification of his researches into the past life of Dimitrios had been that he was making an impersonal experiment in detection. The experiment must not be allowed to become an obsession. He had found out some interesting things about the man. Honour should be satisfied. And it was high time he got on with the book. He had his living to earn and no amount of information about Dimitrios and Mr. Peters or anyone else would compensate for a lean bank balance six months hence. [2]

But regardless of this turn of events, Latimer continues to discover that the world of the imagination and the real world of detection can often become muddled, so that at times it becomes difficult to decipher one from the other. After meeting the millionaire recluse Mr. Grodek in his Geneva home, Latimer writes Mr. Marukakis, somewhat excitedly explaining to him that there are such things as "master spies" of whom no one knows.[3] This is an example of Ambler's military background informing his story telling.

Having served as a member of the British Royal Artillery Regiment as a corporal (also called a bombardier during World War II), Ambler manages to use a great deal of worldly language in his work. A further reference to the relationship between literature and reality takes place when Latimer asks Mr. Grodek if he had ever read any spy stories. Grodek, the master spy who is also simply

---

1. *A Coffin for Dimitrios.* p. 124.

2. Ibid. Latimer's astonishment in discovering that there are "such real people that no ones knows" about is a fine example of the dialectical play that exists between appearance and reality. At this point Latimer's mind begins to reel with the greater understanding that, if this is true in this case, there must be further deceptions or discoveries waiting out there, as well.

3. Ibid., p. 125.

known as "G," answers in the negative and stresses the fact that spy stories seem too naïve to him. The narrator intervenes, stating, "but providence is never quite as calculating as himself and Dimitrios. It may bludgeon away at a man, but it never feels between his ribs with a knife."[1]

The theme of providence versus chance is a paradoxical one in Ambler's writing. On one hand, Latimer happens to be at the right place at the right time. This, of course, can be viewed in the reverse depending on our point of contention. Having been present at Madame Chavez's home, he met Colonel Haki. But was this providence or mere chance? This is precisely the kind of questions that Ambler brings to his work.

It seems to me that traditionally thinkers have answered this kind of question by looking at the outcome. Often enough, we see that when the outcome is a regrettable one, chance is dealt the responsibility. But on occasions when the result of a given event is favorable, providence is invoked. Eric Ambler is cognizant of this dichotomy and inconsistency in our quest for praise. Ambler's mixture of providence and chance is never a simple matter, however. The lines of delineation that bisect providence and chance are often not as sharp as one may think. We can, I suppose, compare the plight of Latimer in some degree to that of a Greek tragedy. Of course, my point here is one of degree and not necessarily one of kind. Latimer, after all, can be rather indiscreet as he meddles in situations of a non-jovial nature. In other words, real world murder and intrigue is no game at all. For this very reason, the Colonel is neither entertained nor moved by these criminal occurrences, while Latimer, who remains a detached onlooker up to the very end of the novel, becomes interested. Latimer's indiscretion, like, perhaps, all forms of indiscretion, is always a case of shortsightedness. Latimer is only concerned with the next sentence that he writes and not with the next real world victim. Thus, regardless of his good will, his noble character, or some other virtues that Latimer may possess,

---

1. Ibid., p. 155.

his indiscretions are rarely granted a second chance. This brings to mind the last chorus in Sophocles' *Ajax*, where the chorus says, "What men have seen they know; but what shall come hereafter no man before the event can see, nor what end waits for him."[1]

Moreover, the question of providence versus chance suggests a meddling with an outcome that may prove to be too utterly overwhelming for Latimer. Let us then ask: what exactly is Latimer hoping to learn about Dimitrios? Assuming that he is not only interested in Dimitrios's life as a kind of game or sport, what is his justification for continuing, after his search has shown some of its hidden hazards? In this regard, the seemingly irreverent Nietzsche, pondering the question of the will to truth, can help us:

> Indeed we come to a long halt at the question about the cause of this will — until we finally came to a complete stop before a still more basic question. We asked about the value of this will. Suppose we want truth: why not rather untruth? And uncertainty? even ignorance? [2]

The seduction and romance of seeking for that which will possibly always remain beyond our grasp remains a strong motivation in human behavior. It is perhaps the single greatest reason most people read. Regardless of the genre, literature allows us to live in a world of the imagination, which often employs conventions that we accept only reluctantly. Literature is often a hazy and eloquent mirror to life itself, which is more often than not untidy, disorganized, and unforeseeable. Kingsley Amis, a writer who tried very hard to demonstrate that serious writers and thinkers do not have to come across as pedantic and serious all of the time, writes in his insightful study of the work of Ian Fleming that literature is a consummate source of excitement because it

---

1. Sophocles. *Ajax.* p. 62.
2. Friedrich Nietzsche. *Beyond Good and Evil: Prelude to a Philosophy of the Future.* Translated by Walter Kaufmann. New York: Vintage Press, 1966. p. 9. The notion of seeking truth, Nietzsche argues, can be misleading given the complexity of what it can reveal. One wonders what it truly is that Latimer attempts to know about Dimitrios. His game playing has consequences that he probably has not pondered.

mirrors our individual temperaments. About the seduction of adventure, Amis writes,

> Let me hark back now to my remark about the universality of the secret-agent figure as a focus for daydreaming. I have no psychological training, so I can only tentatively suggest that what I will call the secret-agent fantasy is marked by being totally portable. Even the keenest fantasist will find that the amount of vicarious life he can get through books and films and television is limited. There come times when none of these is available. He may then look around his environment for some peg to hang his fantasy on, some real starting point for his excursion into unreality. [1]

The point here is not so much the value of literature as therapeutic escapism as it is the fact that most people read for enjoyment. But enjoyment itself does not necessarily preclude either seriousness or prescriptive meaning. Greek tragedies are not exactly light in their themes. However, readers and theatergoers alike take delight in the construction of the work itself, the subtle and the not so subtle truths that these works allude to. But few people take great enjoyment from a "piling-up" of bodies as some critics have called these works. Latimer is a perfect case in point because we are reading a work which is about a reader, in this case one who is also a writer who attempts to leap beyond the bounds of his daily routine. Latimer wants to taste what it would be like to live out what he writes. The drama truly begins when he becomes confused by the fine line that separates the dual realms of appearance and reality, subject and object.

In Chapter Ten, Latimer is surprised to find out that Mr. Peters is really named Petersen, and was a member of Dimitrios' drug-

---

1. Kingsley Amis. *The James Bond Dossier: Is He in Hell or is He in Heaven — that Damned Elusive 007?* New York: The New American Library, 1965. p. 4. Amis' point about needing to "escape" if only momentarily from reality fits in very nicely with Nietzsche's contention that perhaps we do not understand what it would mean for human beings to desire the truth and, this, all of the time. Antonio Caso (1983-1946) equally views our desire to create (art as disinterest) as originating in a vital excess that finds an outlet in embracing intellectual, aesthetic and spiritual values. See: Antonio Caso, *La existencia como economía, desinterés y como caridad*, 1916.

peddling gang. This is the point in the work when Latimer's confidence builds. He sheds some of the artistic conventions that have hitherto kept him in the world of fiction. But he is still no match for the criminally-experienced Mr. Petersen. Latimer lacks the know-how to make him an effective player in the underworld. But the true climax of the work, that is, the decisive moment when the inherent tension in the drama unfolds, takes place in Chapter Twelve. In this chapter Mr. Petersen informs Latimer that Dimitrios is alive and is now known to go by the alias of Monsieur C.K. The man whom Latimer saw in the morgue with Colonel Haki was named Manus Visser; he was wearing Dimitrios' *carte d'identité*. This forces Latimer to reflect on the nature of good and evil, one night when he finds himself in his hotel room unable to sleep. He reflects:

> But it was useless to try to explain him in terms of good and evil. They were no more than baroque abstractions. Good Business and Bad Business were the elements of the new theology. Dimitrios was not evil. He was logical and consistent; as logical and consistent in the European jungle as the poison gas called Lewiste and the shattered bodies of children killed in the bombardment of an open town.[1]

Latimer is clearly out of place in the criminal underworld. He is "like a person who has strayed into a museum for shelter from the rain."[2] At this point, Latimer becomes confused. Literature is no longer something that he can control; instead, it is now a reality that rules over him. Finding himself in a predicament, Latimer naturally begins to feel that the game is over for him. The entire experiment has turned out to be a nightmare. The sensible thing to do now, he reasons, is to call the police. The narrator explains:

---

1. *A Coffin for Dimitrios.* p. 230.
2. Ibid., p. 229. The metaphor of the person that has "strayed into a museum" is very useful in conveying Ambler's earlier notion that it is highly dissatisfying to Latimer that people like himself should have occasion to run into the likes of Dimitrios Makropoulos. This metaphor is an insightful literary device that has the effect of describing a metaphysical reality: chance.

He was left with a choice. Either he could go back to Athens and leave Peters to make the best deal he could with Dimitrios or he could stay in Paris to see the last act of the grotesque comedy in which he now found himself playing a part.[1]

This metaphor of "straying into a museum for shelter from the rain" once again brings to light the theme of appearance and reality and the subjective distance that often separates the two. At this point Latimer's mind, reeling with uncertainty, can only make allusions to a film he once saw and not to reality proper. The denouement finds Latimer and Mr. Petersen sitting in a semi dark hotel room awaiting the arrival of Dimitrios, who has been blackmailed into paying them both a million francs. When Latimer sees Dimitrios for the first time, he is surprised to realize that the criminal is not what he expected. Dimitrios's demeanor is calm and collected. He displays great acumen and ingenuity in matters of the underworld, even though Mr. Petersen has some reservations as to just how intelligent he truly is when he utters, "Ingenuity is never a substitute for intelligence, you know."[2] This is an important point that should not go unnoticed because Amber is suggesting that formal logic is perhaps no more than a series of clever and ingenious mental exercises that cannot be justified in the real world, where causal conditions cannot always be predicted.

At this point Dimitrios shoots both men, even though Petersen manages to get several shots off that mortally wound Dimitrios. As Dimitrios goes down, gasping for breath, he says, "In the end, one is always defeated by stupidity. If it is not one's own it is the stupidity of others."[3] This statement, I believe, is the real rhyme and reason of

---

1. Ibid. p. 226.
2. Ibid. p. 268.
3. Ibid. p. 272. It is rather interesting to note that in the end it is Dimitrios who bemoans the fact that irrational acts, stupidity is actually what he says, should always be what derails human existence. This point conveys Ambler's notion that chance may be a greater reality in human life than providence. This is also another presentation of the misfortune that chance forces man to undergo, except that now this notion of chance is elaborated by Dimitrios.

this novel. Amber leaves the greatest shards of uncertainty and skepticism concerning the nature of reason to the lips of a life-long criminal. We must remember that Dimitrios has also spent a life of planning and deciphering how best to understand the portion of reality that he has chosen to embrace.

The novel is brought to a resounding dialectical conclusion, one that witnesses Latimer writing an explanatory letter to his friend Marukakis. In the letter Latimer is attempting to make sense of his entire ordeal, but now he showcases a newly won wisdom concerning the affairs of the real world and the place of subjectivity in this objective logos. He implies that he has become more confounded than ever before "by the difference between the stupid vulgarities of real life and the ideal existence of the imagination."[1] He can now return to writing without owing alliance to the troublesome illusion that reason, imagination, and reality have anything to do with each other, as far as literature is concerned. These conditions, he argues in his letter will continue to obtain as long as, "might is right, and while chaos and anarchy masquerade as order and enlightenment."[2]

---

1. Ibid., p. 279.
2. Ibid., p. 280.

CHAPTER 2. PILLARS OF REMEMBRANCE: THE PLIGHT OF AESTHETIC VISION AND MORAL COURAGE IN THE MODERN WORLD

> The romance of conscience has been dried up into the science of ethics; which may well be called decency for decency's sake, decency unborn of cosmic energies and barren of artistic flower. — G.K. Chesterton

Vitally conscious observers of human reality cannot fail to observe that time tramples human existence into oblivion. The existentially reflective being exercises the luxury of contemplating eternity momentarily — only while blood streams through our temples, or as long as our free will permits. Thus, mankind always finds itself in a sinister and deceptive present that is constantly fleeting — ever elusive. And along with this passing temporal reality also goes man's lived vision of reality, a vision whose totality, regrettably, we always take with us to the grave. Human existence is differentiated from other forms of life through this utterly subjective and vitally felt inward vision. This existential autonomy forces us to recognize that time acts as a slow moving stream that rides us along its incessant flow toward death. But this subjective autonomy is felt by everyone as a unique and personalized set of circumstances that, regardless of its apparent insignificance in lieu of objective structures, nevertheless remains unsubstantiated from outside the reality that is the self.

Hence, human mortality can never be experienced as a collective reality. Instead, it is always and everywhere felt as a vitally concrete and personally differentiated phenomenon, regardless of what medical materialism may assert. No two human deaths are alike precisely because no two human lives are interchangeable. This very basic cosmic fact serves as the foundation of the truism that the greatest and most sovereign of man's prerogatives is that everyone must die alone. In spite of the ideal closeness and self-understanding that it may exhibit to itself, human existence cannot be viewed as anything less than a cosmic phenomenon. Our proximity to our self — that is, to that fleeing reality that fashions its existence into a fluid and continuous attempt at auto-knowledge, is always an attempt to grasp life as auto-recognition, or self-consciousness. Liberating as this conscious inward gaze might be, it nevertheless points an arrow at the ontological origin that we seek to reveal to ourselves. But if time tramples human reality into forgetfulness, this is nonetheless a painfully and consciously experienced oblivion. Being conscious of our possible future states of being places us at the mercy of a reality that is in some respects already other than what we are at present. This anticipatory conscious reality carries with it a dual role: present and future modes of being. To exist as a future-oriented entity, as Dilthey has pointed out, liberates us from a sub par biologism in which our imagination refuses to become imprisoned.

After seemingly endless treatises and analyses man continues to exist as a being that must bear the responsibility of freedom for itself, a being whose entire creative existence is marked by the desire to rise above the level of a mere biological entity. This instinctual metaphysical vision keeps our primal freedom from being downplayed or dismissed altogether through objectifying superstructures. This subjective freedom is presented as an immediate existential condition whereby, even in a positivistic age, a reflective being can isolate his life to a willed, possible existence. Yet this proactive future that is organized through reflection and that is fashioned in the present cannot be said to exist in itself. Man is always a projection of himself. This is perhaps what is meant by imagination. To negate the fact that imagination is a guiding principle in human freedom is tantamount to living in a permanent present, like a young child.

On the contrary, this possible future to some degree manages to frame our present. Some clear-cut examples of this occur in preventive medicine, for instance. Medical science cannot negate its visionary appeal to anticipate disease and the conditions that allow for its manifestation. Perhaps for this very reason, to purchase a ticket to next week's performance of *La Bohème* in no way guarantees that I will be alive to witness this work or that the opera will even take place. Yet this temporally prescriptive reality springs from the very temporal essence of human existence.

But being aware of our future existential condition can also serve as a form of shackles for some people. The complex metaphysical dynamics of human existence often go undetected by most people. One strong reason for this is that, for many, to live in the present simply means to preclude any such metaphysical underpinning of human reality. Merely satisfying the vegetative drive is tantamount to bliss for many people. The reasonable comfort and immediacy of the present can work to distract us from seeing through this illusorily drawn-out static reality. This condition allows for the passage of vital time to go unnoticed and, what is even more devastating to human existence — even unfelt. This is easily assessed by closely studying what time means for a young child, a type of being who lives in an eternal present. But the heaviness of lived time eventually takes off its cloak, as it were, and in so doing reveals the transient nature of all things human.

Doubtless, the problems faced by this "empirical" subject, as some commentators like to refer to man, are always — regardless of the myopia of the aforementioned positivism — of an internal reality. The life that is fully lived from the inside out beckons the thinker to confront his own reality prior to any decisive clash that may ensue between the subjective part of him and objectifying forces. This creates a buffer zone between my subjective "I" and external reality.

A person who has a finely tuned melancholic sensitivity for the passage of time does not take the lead from seasonal or chronological pressures. The small child is already capable of, and willing to, view himself as a dynamic entity, in spite of the newness of the reality that he is to himself. Kant is correct in saying that time is an a priori reality that the subject intuits. This is easily proven, not through what is often an artificial argumentative stance but through a lived vitality.

The sober understanding that ours is always a solitary death is precisely what binds and solidifies our life as an existential reality. But this inevitable and eventual subjective gaze inward cannot help but take place due to the detached and effacing objectivity that the cosmic phenomena represents. Man finds himself alone, but this solitary reality is also framed by an overbearing cosmic structure that cannot be conceived as anything less than the sublime measure of all things. Following in the footsteps of the ancient Greek thinkers, we come to the realization that what has always been at stake in philosophical reflection is the situating of the subject in the grand logos of the universe.

Perhaps we can even say that this flowing of time that culminates in our eventual death is nothing other than the temporal allowance that death concedes to life for the running of the latter's course. This is said to be the case because limitation is always at the heart of what it means to be human. Human mortality cannot be separated from consciousness and the awareness of time that the latter enables us to develop. Death is perhaps better understood not so much as something that occurs to us, but rather as something that we embody. But given that death resides deep within the corridors of this very life that we possess, we can perhaps also argue that the time of our lives — this vitally intuited time, this lived immediacy that momentarily robs death of its stranglehold on us, also exists in equal proportion to the time that it takes death to bubble up to the surface of life.

The paradoxical nature of human mortality is that while we have all heard rumors, felt the roar of distant innuendos, and even felt the bite of this unpleasant termination to the lives of our loved ones, no one can say with any degree of certainty that he has witnessed death firsthand. Writers have written endless tomes on death and dying and undoubtedly will continue to do so. This seems the only viable possibility for a type of being that requires answers to the antinomies of life. Philosophers, too, have taken apart this subject with surgical precision. But, regardless, to say something constructive about this reality is always tantamount to speaking in the first person, as anything short of this recoils into abstraction and self-indulgent intellectualizing. The collective appeal to discuss death allows us to make greater sense of this fundamental aspect in the life of man. This round table approach to this most personal concern manages to assuage some of our fears and dread concerning the unknown. But, like so many things human, over-analysis and discussion only work to take away the vitality and closeness of reality for those who live on what is felt and intuited. Death may make its appearance as something that sets itself up for reflection and discussion, but death makes itself known as an event only to the dying; the rest are merely spectators to this human drama. And yet, we go through great strides to cheat this, our only certainty.

But if time and death do indeed trample all human identity into oblivion despite our spirited protests, what viable recourse remains open to man? And, if this is truly the logos of human reality, as can be affirmed by a quick glance at the architecture of all things human, where does man's reservoir of meaning lie? Spatial temporal reality shows its teeth in the eternal supply of transience that dislocates the axis of man's sense of reality. Is this perhaps why man comes to feel world-weary? If this is the case, then the matter becomes even more complicated because perhaps it demonstrates that man has traditionally done nothing other than to negate this cosmic factum.

The public and seemingly more familiar face of the task of seeking meaning in human existence is often sought in collective or community structures and institutions. Church and state come to mind as formidable examples of this kind. But the ultimate stamp of necessity in this task is always an inscrutably personal and thus private one. One reason for this is because subjectivity always finds itself in a situation that is original to its very essence as an instance of individuality. Finding himself in a fluid present, man instinctually attempts to hold on to ready-made rules. Familial reality is a central and formative component of human existence; this circumstance aids the individual in finding a place for himself that is commensurate with his blossoming perspective. The prerogative of subjectivity is that of fashioning or discovering a logos that is flexible enough to embrace the role of the subject-I in what is often an unbending and objectifying realm that suffocates genuine subjectivity. The individual must learn to listen to this subjective calling and to embrace its inherent autonomy. Existential subjectivity ought never to isolate itself from the contingencies of reality. On the contrary, human autonomy demands logical rigor and sincerity. As a consequence the great degree of heterogeneity exhibited by human existence cannot easily be substituted by depersonalized objective measures. Every man re-creates the world, as a vital affirmation of lived-existence.

The fiercely independent and philosophically irreverent Albert Camus (1913-1960) seems to have captured the essence of this realization best — the realization of human life itself, even — when he wrote in *The Myth of Sisyphus* that for two men who live the same number of years, the world will allow them the very same number of experiences. However, the manner in which we may become conscious of this vital seasoning will depend solely on our individual will. Camus seems to imply (correctly, I will argue) that human existence is always fashioned from differences in moral quality and never as a matter of quantity, and this in regard to autonomy. Camus' great treatise of man vis-à-vis the absurd is a triumph of the will over all that is objectifying and demoralizing in human life.

A close and careful reading of *The Myth of Sisyphus* and *The Rebel* bears this out. In these works Camus argues that subjectivity seeks its own understanding, but instead discovers that only an infinite abyss exists. What, then, is left for man to do? Camus' stoical and ironical answer to this existential conundrum is his understanding that a being that demands such explanations to life's complexities is also one who simultaneously finds some semblance of meaning in the asking. Thus he writes, "being aware of one's life, one's revolt, one's freedom, and to the maximum, is living, and to the maximum."[1]

This optimum living, this insufferable yet curious joie-de-vivre is nothing other than the exercise of imagination in the service of life. This is a manner of protesting the very workings of the cosmic phenomenon that quietly tramples human existence. Of course, Camus' reflective and lyrical logic has an advantage over more analytically-inclined thinkers in that his philosophical works demonstrate a vital ground that ought to be a central component of all works of philosophy. Part of his success in this project is that he presents this confrontation with life as a fluidly dynamic first-person account of reality. His analysis of life never strays from the essence of the vital immediacy that is differentiated personal existence. One responsibility that his readers face is to extrapolate this message. Camus' major metaphysical contention simply comes down to something like: "Here we find ourselves, stranded on material soil. Now, what is one to do?" To this question (which he finds to be naïve), his answer is tantamount to: "Live... and live with moral courage! What else?" Ortega, too, equally argues that to live is to view life as an existential preoccupation. However, Ortega does

---

1. Albert Camus. *The Myth of Sisyphus*. p. 63. The true meaning of Camus' notion of metaphysical rebellion is the situating of man in the cosmos as what Ortega calls a cosmic phenomenon. Camus is of the firm belief that viable answers to the questions of human existence are not necessarily found in social-political structures, but rather serves as a meditation on the nature of the self.

not posit that life is absurd, but rather that Camus' contention of the absurd, too, is a moral fabrication. The primal make-up of human existence, Ortega argues, is not for humans to judge.

But the response that Camus offers in light of the cosmic order of things is his manner of stating that, even if life is indeed trampled by time, man nevertheless retains the right to review this process. This is the true meaning of metaphysical rebellion, then.

Now, I suppose that this self-conscious and appropriating volition that knows the object and direction of its own willing is a kind of vital noblesse oblige where we owe ourselves the responsibility of self-knowledge. Thus, Socrates' notion that the unexamined life is not worth living is much more than the idiosyncrasy of an old man. Instead, this is the recognition that self-understanding becomes the central axis from which all subsequent understanding is possible. But this is precisely what nobility means in the first place: the existential hunger and desire to allow our will to act in accordance with our virtue, or what is still a greater force, with our vocation. The main difficulty in this realization, however, lies in arriving at the timely wisdom that this search inevitably takes the path of most resistance. In addition, the intuition of time also heightens our sense of personal destiny. But resistance and limitation are only one side of the strife that we encounter in human life as an existential drama that begs for a director.

Socrates' evolution from pondering questions about the natural order into questions of moral subjectivity is precisely the grounding that delineates between the philosopher and the scientist, for instance. This is perhaps why the genuine and holistic culmination of philosophy as a way of life is found in the existential thought of the stoics and not with overly analytical renditions of human historicity. The latter possibility has always been the quick and ready approach to solving human questions through abstractions. But this transient and historicist overview is never more than a covering up the complexities of space and time with a canvas of local historical color. Time and space may showcase a historical importance to some thinkers, but there is no denying the reality that both of these superstructures presuppose the same existential preoccupation for all in one-way or other.

Camus, as well as most contemplative thinkers of the last two millennia, shared this universally vital attitude toward life. Thus, the categorical imperative of philosophical reflection becomes synonymous with the notion that any philosophy worth justifying should also be one worth living.

But if reflection on experience only takes place after the fact, what realistic chance do we ever have of appropriating our true existential possibilities? Also, coupled with this dilemma is the overwhelming and dynamic nature of time itself. The relentless grip of time on human existence does not allow us the luxury to experiment with many vital options while still retaining an autonomous authenticity. Human existence is not a laboratory where we can readily discard failed options. Instead, if human existence is to enjoy an overall stability and cohesion it can achieve this through a proactive vision. Thus, while reflection on experience remains a viable manner of attaining understanding, this alone cannot be the guiding principle of human existence. What is essential as a vital guide for human existence is forward-looking, intuitive contemplation. But this condition does not apply to those who presuppose that reflection is merely an empirically conditioned phenomenon. However, if we believe that mind is active and prescriptive in composition we must assume accountability for our own lived awareness of the passage of time — this, in lieu of our eventual timeless obscurity. Success in this process requires an aesthetic visionary stance toward our existence that transforms all future subjectivity into a lived autonomy — that is, into an objective subject of its own choosing.

The consumption of the atomic structure of time, in the form of the vital time that makes up our life, is the paramount question of human existence. In good will, we can attest that there is no greater concern for human existence. Yet this question also boils down to one of perspective. The passage of time serves as a mirror to the fluidity of our life, that is, to subjectivity as the latter confronts or comes to term with itself. As such, the passage of time is the main objectification of man. But maintaining a clear perspective, much like poetic sensibility, for instance, is not an obvious characteristic of man. This very question can propel us either to action — that is, to cultivate a greater awareness of ourselves — or it can equally paralyze our will in the absence of any existential aspirations. Lacking any aspirations to the metaphysical fertility that defines human existence, our lives become no more than banal and obscure representations of the life of others. In such cases we become caricatures of each other: everyman seeking the anonymity that he values in material reality. But by the same token, a person who cannot witness his own differentiation from the stale grip of nature can never aspire to a greater grounding to his existence than that found in a second rate surrealist comedy. This kind of tragic scenario, we come to recognize, is the greatest of human aberrations. For instance, this same sentiment is substantiated in Italo Svevo's novel *Confessions of Zeno*, when the main character states, "I seem to be able to see my thought as something quite apart from myself."[1]

One of the most interesting aspects of time, as we humans live it, I will argue, has to do with its uncharted, unpredictable, and untamable core characteristics. Both time and life exhibit the central condition that comes most natural to the ass: an unfettered defiance. Man, in his most naïve and natural circumstance, merely finds himself helplessly swept along such a temporal current. Thus faced with such an abstinent predicament, what then ought we to do?

There is no doubt that man — that is, the differentiated life of every one of us — is today, yesterday, and will remain tomorrow caught between infinite time and our own conscious grasp of this central contradiction in human consciousness. Human existence cannot be separated from the reality that time poses for subjectivity. For this reason Georg Simmel writes that: "Time is the form of

---

1. Italo Svevo. *Confessions of Zeno.* p.3.

consciousness of that which constitutes life itself in its immediate concreteness, and which cannot be enunciated, but only lived; it is life stripped of its contents."[1] This is not another theory, but rather a sheer and unadulterated matter of fact. The problem is that some people never seem to capture the essence of time as a lived phenomenon unless it is qualified in the form of an itinerant activity. But what can we do with mere facts once our understanding revolts and arrives at the timely understanding that reason ought to be a vital tool at the service of life? The facticity of human mortality is such a fact. But how can an overabundance of clinically cold facts come to our aid in a materialist and technological age? We ought not to allow ourselves to be fooled by facts, but learn to use them as tools for life. In addition, the usefulness of facts should allow us to encapsulate them in a vital approach to human existence that helps to liberate our understanding from objectification.

Remembrance, too, is one of those very unitary facts of human consciousness. But remembrance is also an essential tool in understanding ourselves. For this same reason remembrance must keep pace with temporal succession. Remembrance, then, becomes the residue of time that has become internalized. Thus, remembrance can never become idle. To remember a face from long ago, a timeless childhood feeling for the people, places and things that surround us, and to grapple with our own mortality can never be swept aside with an empty, overly pragmatic gaze. Such acts of remembrance are a measure of lived reality and never a matter of idle speculation. The difference between these two is witnessed in the detached interest that we take when rummaging through the objects on display at an estate sale, for instance. That home, those objects, and the memories contained within those walls do not belong to us, and as such they do not exist for us. Hence existence, as manifested through subjectivity, can never be a simple and stale

---

1. Julián Marías. *History of Philosophy*. New York: Dover Publications, Inc. 1966. p. 386. Simmel's contention that time is life stripped of its contents is also what Ortega means by life as narrative. Narrative or drama, he tells us, is the phenomenon of time and life as these manifest themselves to me, but which strictly speaking do not constitute my life.

recognition of matters of fact. The prospective buyer at the estate sale does not encounter the life of the deceased as a fact, only as a vague character in a fictional world. To ascertain the vitality that the deceased possess for themselves requires at least two things: a good will, and the recognition of the lived vitality that we are to ourselves. But this is a process of imagination — of extrapolation; and, as such, a matter of existential effort. Externally viewed, then, there is nothing utterly factual about the inner constitution of an existential being — one that consciously situates itself in the order of time. What is so utterly "factual" about recognizing oneself to exist and to later perish? Can this same being come to acknowledge a timely futility in all of its works? There is no precedent for such a self-conscious notion anywhere else in nature. We reflect and seek remembrance because we are coerced to extend — in point of fact, to stretch the finite moments that deprive us of a projected vital eternity. Therefore the main work of consciousness is to remember that subjectivity, as a factum of our own existence cannot subject itself to scrutiny forever, only as long as it is vitally felt. This is a clear indication of the gulf that exists between theory and life.

Hence, I will argue that aesthetic vision and moral courage are the twin badges that adorn the pillars of remembrance. Intuitive vitality, that is, the condition where we sustain our life by the use of our imagination, is often felt as a tremor that moves us from within. The realization that all human existence is a death-defying romance, one that is felt as an intuition of reality, is also an affirmation of human existence as narrative. This narrative of which I speak is a life that is vibrantly felt from the inside out, as Ortega has so aptly argued. Every human life is seen as a present reality from an objective point of view. Hence, from the outside, the life of human beings is seen as being no different than that of other lower forms of life. This, of course, is where the myopia and bankruptcy of materialism is felt the strongest. Whenever we encounter another person we only witness the present condition of that individual. We cannot experience all the other "presents" that that person has been or has embodied. Yet other past "present" moments inform our very being. Inwardly, this subjectivity knows nothing else but its past or what amounts to its self-identity. In contradistinction to this condition, we tend not to notice the effects of the passage of time on our body. Thus if the world-at-large enlists our moral sympathy, this can only come about through an inwardly felt attitude about our life and what the passage of time means to our mortality. To reflect and care for our existential constitution signifies that an authentic connection has been established with a vital characteristic of our being. Only after we arrive at such an understanding can our lives become tied to the "maximum" condition that Camus has so well described. Anything short of this self-embracing amor-fati falls to the level of nihilism, in any of its variegated forms.

In addition, moral courage is a vital condition that is felt from within. Moral courage paints a picture of man as a tragic hero. Again, we must stress that the imminent danger on which our lives are perpetually hinged can only be understood by an act of imagination. Imagination always comprehends the inner workings of the vital danger that surrounds human existence. As such, imagination also recognizes the limitations of our will. This sincerity, stated in a few bold words, is the essence of being in touch with reality. Where this imagination is lacking, life, too, tramples remembrance into oblivion. But any time that remembrance is absent as an existential gauge, self-conscious existence cannot take place. Remembrance is a humane path that liberates, that classifies and also obfuscates, and that can offer salvation. Ironically, salvation comes about as the result of envisioning our future vital tranquility.

The central existential-anthropological question remains quite open as to how many people are ever up to this task? Thus, it seems that remembrance and wisdom always go together. But who wants to remember? Who ought to remember? Remembrance is dead weight, we hear some critics say. When Rudolph Carnap and other members of the Vienna Circle, the philosophical school that emphasized the clarification of language over metaphysical reality attempted to embrace axiology, they did so by favoring "progressive" values because the reasoning was that conservative ones kept the past alive.

Progressive critics have underscored the need to move on and to embrace the present, if not the future. But what these critics consider to be the good or liberating essence of future values, always remain incomplete without recourse to a historically sound rooting in the past. Moreover, materialist critics can be heard asking: What are the margins, parameters, and possibilities that time and life leave for such a vital act of remembrance? Between a life replete with action, reaction, and further corrective action what vital desire is left for remembrance? Why attribute such importance to these bourgeois notions, they seem to say. Or is it perhaps that this business-as-usual regimen is precisely the spiteful condition that shuns a life of remembrance?

It seems that human life is framed by two equally absurd notions: Being and Non-being. For he who "exists" and makes nothing of it, there can never be the kind of dilemma of which I am writing. But to fully understand that "I am now" and yet that "I will not be" any longer in a given time in the future only leaves us with a paradoxical belief that we life forever. This momentary illusion occurs for the perplexing reason that we never encounter our own death. Instead, what we do find is that we are "immortal" for as long as we live. This may seem like a contradiction in terms, but on closer inspection we realize that life is all that we know. Death is only encountered in anticipation.

On the other hand, this present moment, this lived-time, embodies the totality of all the other future moments to come. The anticipation of death guides us in our actions as much as life itself. But we are also faced with the reality that time itself cannot be tamed. This uncertainty, however, only leaves us with a bitter, humbling taste on our palates. Finite as our intuition of the immediacy of our lives may be, we nonetheless must allow our acuity to develop by taking an active role in our intuitive vision of lived-time. Thus, if this is our greatest and most pressing vital task, as I have been arguing, then what else is there for us mortals to do?

Thus, a life lived with one eye turned to our mortality and the other to the dual virtues of aesthetic vision along with moral courage rounds out our subjective nature with the acceptance of our grounding in an objective, spatial-temporal reality. Aesthetic vision calls for the realization that human existence is no less than a possible artistic enterprise. But such a solemn enterprise can only be enacted by an equally intuitively felt notion of spirit. Thus, Dilthey is correct in his placing of auto-gnosis at the head of all philosophical activity. This vitally-felt reality that the Spanish philosopher Jose Ortega y Gasset called the ultimate and hence "radical reality" makes human subjectivity into a kind of narrative lyricism. For thinkers who share a vital imagination, this ideal also serves as an intuitive aesthetic of time. We can argue that the existence of the self can only be experienced internally through the realization of finding itself as an alien at the center of the material realm. This process is dialectical in scope because the objectifying presence of the material realm forces the thinker back into himself. However, such a reality does not necessarily have to become encapsulated in its own subjectivity as some critics have argued. This experience, when fully realized, re-focuses, and refreshes our orientation to the material world with its myriad array of representations. Any conscious desire for auto-reflection necessarily directs our gaze back towards the objective realm. To find ourselves smack in the middle of these material phenomena is also to come to terms with the dualistic nature of human existence. Only from this feebly rooted material reality — this biological human life, as some people insist on calling it — can a truly self-conscious and redeeming human existence arise.

In other words, man finds himself amongst a multitude of "others" and only then decides that he must make sense of such a reality. Human existence or what amounts to the differentiated life of every one of us is an irrefutable "fact" that is always understood and verified from the inside out. This raw condition is no less than the initial factum of human existence, as the former comes to know itself.

This thought brings to mind T.S. Eliot's concluding words in his poem *East Coker*, "In my end is my beginning." The beginning, then, ironically is always a vital choice that sheds light over an inevitable and relentless end. This intuitive vision for which I am deliberating garners our ability to create something like an aesthetic existence out of our life. Human life always begins with the same primal raw conditions: an individual born into a maddening cluster of material reality, one that includes other life forms that surround it. These are the facts as we know them. But this minimalist and innocuous truism ought not to confuse or disorient us. Our task as reflective beings is to develop a genuine self-embracing consciousness, that is to say, self-consciousness. We become alerted to this reflective task through what is often an ephemeral internal condition that is fomented through recognition of our individual vocation. Accordingly, we can argue that such a vital condition draws attention to itself through an inquietude that cannot help but to become manifested as a conscious yearning to come to terms with material reality. Thus human existence can never be a mere biological reality. Human existence, in addition, is understood as a conscious, quasi-natural phenomenon as Ortega has described.

In this very same measure, we realize that our moral courage, on the other hand, is a vehement response to the ever objectifying and dehumanizing process that is raw nature in its vilest form. Thus, moral courage is forged through our ability to become who our latent aspirations confront us with. However, on the other hand we cannot deny that we must face a relentless and often asphyxiating material reality like universal history without simultaneously falling prey to an inane historicism. Human existence, that is, subjective consciousness first confronts itself — in the instances when it does so — with what can be considered its opposite, material reality. The physical universe, along with its seemingly endless array of differentiated entities becomes the assemblage for our coming upon the discovery of our self. Our encounter with physical reality serves as the ground for catapulting human life into self-consciousness. The physical world (or the social environment, as some today call this phenomenon) is always the true oasis where consciousness seeks to encounter itself. But this arena alone cannot enact this reflective endeavor. For some, this struggle remains frustrating and often even serves to enrage the moral sensibility into nihilism. But for others the oasis is attainable and even tamable, always showing itself to be nothing other than the bait that helps to snag our self-conscious engagement, as it were.

Thus, notwithstanding any future hypothesis that posits that the seat of consciousness has been discovered, the reflective thinker would greet this pronouncement with a sly smile. Any such hypothesis will probably originate as a further naive and utopian attempt at seeking the perfectibility of man. The result of this will prove to be inimical to any future notion of self-worth in man. Human dignity always comes with a high price. For, what is such a pronouncement to mean to future human freedom? The social-political implications of such a discovery, as the case may be, may prove to be a "liberating" force in the life of those who are life-weary, and who have exhausted their free will. But for the consciously reflective being this pronouncement will serve as a further stumbling-blocking to true moral worth. In the face of such a "discovery," what collectively-oriented mass mentality will confound itself to seek the truth, much less to live it? And what moral convictions must such a pronouncement naturally entail? We are currently witnessing a sampling of this aberrant lack of self-worth in the explosion of elective cosmetic surgery, for instance. Furthermore, what conscientious being would act on this new discovery, wrangled right out of the dictate of empirical thought? The imaginative thinker — who is always faced with the futility of such an arresting development will still be left with the copious and burning sensation that asks whether the discoverers of this new human paradigm would regard this as a free act or as coerced by the very subject of inquiry?

I suppose that if such a pronouncement enters the books as "fact," moral courage, rather than becoming obliterated would only necessitate a re-birth, if not altogether a boost to the allure of human freedom vis-à-vis this vitally extinguishing hypothesis. This, I believe, will prove to be a decisive question for humanity. This concern has greater implications for human freedom than does the notion of cloning, for instance. In cloning we at least know that what we are creating are sub-human beings that have been fabricated in laboratories, often out of a sheer will to challenge nature. But the question of human consciousness threatens to unseat the very essence of what it means to be human by presenting us with a synthetic rendition of human life as a series of related mechanical functions dictated by DNA. Ironically, it does not appear to have dawned on proponents of the latter theory that such a question can only be addressed voluntarily by agents having free will.

Walker Percy begins his novel *Lancelot* by having its protagonist, Lancelot Andrewes, a man who is being held in "the institute for aberrant behavior," utter the following words: "Have you noticed that the narrower the view the more you can see? For the first time I understand how old ladies can sit on their porches for years."[1] A person who finds himself detained in a place like Lancelot must begin to imagine what lies outside the narrow view that is granted him by six-inch slits in the wall. The world that such a being witnesses serves as a frame to that reality that he must extrapolate. In other words, he must see the world through a negation. But this mental act is nothing other than a perpetual act of reflection. Stated in clear terms, this vehement act of imagination upholds the dignity of human existence.

Thus a future that claims to have established a factual understanding of the nature of consciousness will clearly only excite the imaginative thinker to imagine what lies beyond such a limited view. What then? sensitive people will ask (at least while we are still somewhat temporally detached from such a caustic pronouncement). Yet, some will still manage to ask, like the enlightening Polish philosopher, poet, and painter Stanislaw Witkiewicz (1885-1939) in his insightful essay "Metaphysical

---

1. Walker Percy. *Lancelot.* p. 3.

Feelings," how anyone can feel complete without a genuine metaphysical component to their existence?[1] But after such a paradigm begins to gain momentum, that is, once that we find ourselves in the midst of such a reality — when we find ourselves entrenched in the entrails of such a closed historical theory, at that point any comparison with the past will become nothing more than a distant memory. Nor will these concerns possibly matter, to most people, then. Collective memory is a rather tenuous thing. At that time our freedom would have totally been won over by medical materialism. Yet such a time will prove to be the supreme training ground for moral courage.

The ultimate irony in this possible future lies in the fact that in conquering consciousness we will also conquer death. Questions of life and death cannot mean much to a kind of being that, in viewing itself in the mirror, becomes convinced that human existence is nothing other than the result of physical processes. That future status quo would have no use for any acts of remembrance. The ethos of this being, due to its own inner limitations would naturally prevent it from attaining any form of reality that embraces the sublime. Any such paradigm will be moved solely by the dual values of utility and economy of thought. At such a time not only will time trample life, but rather life will negate itself due to its disregard for vital time.[2]

---

1. Stanislaw Witkiewicz. p. 285. Witkiewicz argues that all works of philosophy and literature, that is, all works that require vision and imagination cannot be solely photographic representations of reality. He writes in *Insatiability*: "Life has nothing to do with literature except for writers who have no business being in literature — literal-minded photographers of life's musty little corners. Literature proper — not the theatre and not poetry, but fiction — invents new realities..."

2. Chesterton writes that the age of the specialist confuses the disease with its cure. He writes: "a book of modern social inquiry has a shape that is somewhat sharply defined. It begins as a rule with an analysis, with statistics, tables of population, decrease of crime among Congregationalists, growth of hysteria among policemen, and similar ascertained facts; it ends with a chapter that is generally called 'The Remedy.' It is almost wholly due to careful, solid, and scientific method that 'the Remedy' is never found. For this scheme of medical question and answer is a blunder; the first great blunder of sociology. It is always called for stating the disease before we find the cure. But it is the whole definition and dignity of man that in social matters we must actually find the cure before we define the disease." See: *What's Wrong with the World?* p. 3.

CHAPTER 3. AUTO-GNOSIS, SUBJECTIVITY AND THE ROLE OF MAXIMS IN PHILOSOPHICAL REFLECTION

> Philosophy triumphs over past ills and ills to come,
> but present ills triumph over philosophy.
> — François Duc de La Rochefoucauld

Sitting outside late into the night and staring into the infinitely vast array of star clusters, nebulas, and galaxies the amateur astronomer becomes privy to the sublimity of space and time. But the real joy and beauty of the aforementioned transcends mere scientific respect for the laws of astrophysics. Scientists explain questions of space and time through quantification of one form or other. Yet the fundamentally vital concern in all of this is the realization that the awe and wonder of space and time does not pertain so much to that reality itself, but to the fact that there should be a subject that can fathom such things. To scrutinize this reality in mere scientific terms amounts to a detriment to this particular human experience — making it an incomplete experience, at best. What is the role of the subject in this respect? Instead a broader concern has to do with the vital nature of subjectivity and its relationship to the metaphysics of existential autonomy.

The introspective qualities of this question subsequently lead me to ask: How is it that most works of philosophy (with a few marked exceptions outside the thought of the ancient stoics, and modern thinkers such as Wilhelm Dilthey, Kierkegaard, Nietzsche, and movements like philosophy of life), phenomenology and existentialism have not allotted the question of subjectivity a more prominent role as the seat of differentiated human existence? Historical examples abound where what is addressed is not man as a differentiated cosmic and reflective subject, but rather as a theoretical and elusive collective mankind that, quite frankly, cannot help but to remain faceless. My pre-occupation with this subject matter — that is, my immediate and vital interest here — is not necessarily in understanding the historical whereabouts of mankind — our origins in space and time, our collective sub-conscious or other such commonly held anthropological conceptions of man.

I suppose that there is a place, even a special place, in the history of ideas for a detailed and scientific consideration and treatment of this subject. However, the pressing necessity for today is to recognize that the overwhelming treatment of this question has taken place in an inane positivistic manner. The inability of positivistic theories to recognize man as a transcendent being has played itself out to such a degree that it can longer make sense of individual, differentiated man in a technological age. Today we have the vitally pressing need for an understanding of man that allows for the recognition and further development of man as an autonomous being. Perhaps the greatest irony of our time is that man has never been in greater need of developing a genuinely autonomous personality and self-expression.

If truth is taken into account, I must confess that I have never encountered "man" — at least not in the impersonal, abstracted form of which science, and lately the social sciences speak. Scientific renditions of man have fashioned man into a phantasmagoric specter that no longer recognizes itself. This clay caricature has invaded the sublime places were man once dwelled and in so doing has depleted man's reservoir of meaning in all of its configurations. My concern, then, has to do with subjectivity and how this is embedded in the structure of autonomous persons. The question of subjectivity and individual autonomy can only retain a genuine connection to reality when it is proposed by the subject itself. This activity is no other than the genuine calling forth of personal vocation. Leszek Kolakowski seems to pinpoint the scope of this problem best when he writes in *Modernity on Endless Trial*:

> Those who hate gardening need a theory. Not to garden without a theory is a shallow, unworthy way of life. A theory must be convincing and scientific. Yet to various people various theories are convincing and scientific. Therefore we need a number of theories. The alternative to not-gardening without a theory is to garden. However, it is much easier to have a theory than actually to garden.[1]

On all of my meanderings through the wide world I have managed to meet and converse with many people, each with a particular passion and a story to convey. And, with the exception of ideologues and some overly theorizing, castle-building academics, none of these people recognize their lives — their dreams, fears, and aspirations in the positivistic sketches prepared by the aforementioned. Is that not a genuine disservice to reality itself and to those who find it fruitful to build their lives according to the anchor that human reality offers? And when the worst of theorizing

---

1. Kolakowski, Leszek. *Modernity on Endless Trial*. Chicago: The University of Chicago Press, 1990, p. 240. This quote seems to capture the essence of the cul-de-sac that theory for theory's sake can become. Theoria for the Greeks meant "vision" and "contemplation." This implies that theory cannot be a self-contained, self — referential activity, but rather the end result of a clarity of mind or understanding. Theoria is a vital necessity, not as an end in itself. Francisco Quesada has suggested that the best and most useful theories are those that originate from a vital spontaneity, and not from a pre-fabricated or self-conscious act. See: *Latin American Philosophy in the* Twentieth Century: Man, Values, and the Search for Philosophical Identity. Edited By Jorge J. E. Gracia. Amherst, New York: Prometheus Books, 1986.

has been explicitly refuted by reality, why are we willing to hold on to theories that seem laughable at best and vacuous and destructive at worst? The latent violence that such hollow theorizing has on the spirit of man is degrading and far reaching. This inversion where man's viscera are spilled out onto the street for public verification has made man into a caricature of himself. This has also created a monstrous age when new neuroses are continuously being piled up, one atop of another, some which have even become the very staples of fashion.

The insistence on continuing to argue for man as a failed abstraction — a vacuous creature that few can recognize — has created a modern-day Frankenstein. If it is true that we often find what we seek, then we ought to look no further than to reality itself for genuine understanding. The laboratory scientist, for instance, is engaged in patterns, statistics, commonality, and a generalizing logic. This is undeniably important to those hard sciences that must maintain these presuppositions as objective standards. But can science also benefit from a holistic vision of man? I will argue that this is undoubtedly a foundational condition of both, science as a form of humanism as well as to its practitioners as individuals. Thus, I must reiterate that whatever existentially pressing implications that this question may generate can also be said of people in other disciplines as individuals as well.

Hence, this subjective empathy remains true to itself as long as we envision the concept of "other" as individuals, first. The moment that our understanding of the other becomes collectivized or abstracted, we also lose the thread and importance of this vital concern. This same question cannot be asked of a collective abstraction called "humanity" without also risking losing its meaning altogether. Extrapolation, imagination, and good will are all necessary ingredients when making the transition from the subjective-I to the objective-we. All philosophical reflection, then, ought to confront and concern itself with that which is vitally nearest to man. And without a doubt, what is always nearest to every one of us is our own life as the grounding of what can be termed objective reality. Again, I stress that my initial concern has to do with the nature of subjectivity as this applies to the lived-existential aspect of man, and not with an analytic rendition of what this word may or may not mean. When engaged in reflection on human existential subjectivity one does not want to fall into the same predicament as a dog that, after several dizzying minutes of going in circles after its own tail, finds out that all along there was a dog in the way. Hence to be effective and even conclusive, the question, "What is human existence?" must be posed from a first-person perspective, as anything other than this stance becomes pure pedantry. To find oneself aware of the fact that human life is always a singular event, and to realize that such an event should arrive at a self-conscious recognition, serves as a central and illuminating definition of *philo-sophia.*

I will approach this subject, then, with the reverence and respect for individual manifestations of subjectivity that such a phenomenon merits. This may mean that we must approach the life of the other as a proto-first man, where suspicion and cynicism play no role. Existential man is nothing other than a differentiated cosmic fact. But genuine and unconditional reflection on this conscious cosmic phenomenon is increasingly becoming rare in this technologically impersonal age. There can be no doubt that to open a philosophy journal in this positivistic age is prove enough that this mere auto da fé often leaves one longing for an age when philosophy was synonymous with self-reflection. Perhaps thinkers should undertake to attack philosophical problems with more personal zest, vital zeal, and sincerity, and abandon ideological doctrines, and the positivistic and arid presuppositions set up by the academy. For some thinkers today the very vital distinction that exists between philosophical vocation and mere employment is often blurred or completely ignored in the service of self-gratification and political expediency. So, too, today the gulf between theory and life has never been greater. Also, perhaps an effort can be made to lessen the regard that some contemporary thinkers have for what is often a delusional sense of objectivity that springs from an exaggerated, pathological, and utopian mania for "theory." Such a mania is perhaps a sound indicator of a greater bankruptcy in humanistic thought than some thinkers are willing or capable of admitting. Regardless of the insight and overall value of most philosophical systems, such constructions nevertheless always remain incomplete. However, I must make clear that precision and objectivity in all things human remain a very worthy ideal. Of twentieth-century thinkers, perhaps none is a greater example of the necessity for clarity than the thought of Ortega y Gasset. But, in terms of human existence, this same theoretical "objectivity," when arrived at from the outside only manages to trivialize and obfuscate the nature of personal experience.

This notion of subjectivity and individuality, then, essentially boils down to one of human freedom. Regard for primal human freedom cannot be argued away in overly intellectualized sophisms. Hence, to paraphrase Colin Wilson in his provocative book, *The Outsider*, we can argue that human existential freedom is always best explained in terms of intensity of will. We can also regard will to be the engine that executes and protracts thought in the objective plane.

Thus, the emphasis of this chapter is to attempt to tackle the problem of human subjectivity by borrowing the title from Anais Nin's humble essay on D.H. Lawrence, or what she referred to as, "An Unprofessional Study."[1] It is sufficient for most thinkers to arrive at a position where they can have something objective to say about their own existential concerns, without pretending that they always de facto utter something about mankind. However, the ironic truth of self-reflection is the subsequent value that this activity places on objectivity. An inward-turned philosophical attitude can never evade the need to make sense of the greater external structures in which subjectivity must become grounded. This dualistic tension is part of the inward turn in the first place.

---

1. Nin's title is unassuming and sincere. This is the work of a writer and most importantly of a conscientious reader. It also poses the question: who is best suited to take up the role of critic? p. 55.

Subjectivity is recognized by the dialectical twists and meanderings that self-reflection demands of itself. This truth necessitates reaffirmation, especially today when psychoanalysis and its many derivatives ground understanding on environmental and materialist forces, while denigrating the possibility for self-knowledge. In effect, self-reflection and auto-gnosis have become "unprofessional" areas of study for its adherents. But rather than signifying the breakdown of objectivity, self-reflection instead merely locates our existential vigor in a greater and objectifying realm. Subjectivity, then, exists embedded within this ameliorated objective reality. It is conceivable and even desirable that through personal reflection we do arrive at universal conclusions. But this is achieved through individual and differentiated vital acts of deciphering reality. The search for autonomous subjectivity, which always also means establishing its boundaries, is a vital necessity that seeks transcendence. This process is nothing less than an encounter with the sublime that encompasses human existence and that we must face on our own accord. This is also an example of true heroism.

This solitary trek of existential exegesis is welcomed by those who understand the severity of what is at stake. This activity has traditionally been nothing other than life-seeking self-understanding. After all, arguments, their premises and their conclusion are either accepted or denied by individuals based on their inherent capacity and desire to seek truth. Adherents of truth ought to make no greater claim for it than to view it as a guide for human existence.[1] This is predicated on the fact that human reality is never presented to us as a finished or even a polished coherence. The daily existential toil of having to remake or complete what we started the day before can become overwhelming for some people; and thus some abandon the struggle for self-knowledge altogether. At best, this negation can lead to a form of world-weariness that

---

1. From its earliest days, philosophy has always been a vital tool in the aid of life. By this I mean that even when philosophy attempted to assert some universal truth, it did so from the conviction that we can transcend our human perspective, but only through a Herculean individual effort.

becomes a sort of existential sleepwalking. It is not uncommon to see how cynicism and the loss of will quickly follow.

But what can we offer the hardboiled cynic? How do we satisfy the thirst for debased and formless epistemological uniformity and the denial of individuality that is so rampant in so many of the doctrinal renditions of man that modernity has given rise to? One can address the cynic's incessant quest for anecdotal and quantifiable evidence by stressing the fact that primal human existence is much more demanding in its existential exigencies than what some extraneous and skeptical materialism can muster. Some overly analytic critic may ask, "How do we justify this alleged subjectivity and self-autonomy?" To such individuals — this being the call of a positivistic age — one can suggest that ultimately this anti-humanism does not apply to people involved in self-reflection — that is, to any thinker engaged in the solitary process of auto-gnosis. The reason for this is that the reflective thinker is already pre-disposed through vocation to justify his own subjectivity through the realization that the discovery of subjectivity and genuine self-reflective thought is one and the same thing. A desired goal of personal reflection is the attainment of a form of existential autonomy that is life-affirming and that does not find it necessary to achieve objective verification. Time, life, and human existence are all proof enough of this truism.

For instance, in opposition to this existential reality, it is clear why ideology necessarily limits the autonomy of the individual. The real test of autonomy, however, resides in the ability of a subject to understand the limit that truth itself places on its adherents. This system of checks and balances is an example of understanding that turns its sincere attention to itself.

Furthermore, this question is a reflection of the critic's own inner epistemological inadequacy, which seeks a sophomoric utopian security in creating a system of hyper-verification where perhaps none is forthcoming or warranted. Human existence stubbornly continues to exhibit a central core of "mystery" that necessitates to be addressed equally through exploration of nonrational belief systems. Thus, I would suggest that problems related to subjectivity, that is, questions of the nature of autonomous human existence, cannot be approached, much less "solved," from without. This is so because the vital and central concerns of subjectivity are never abstractions nor are they collective in scope, and as such are not subject to any scientific or positivistic methodological scrutiny. Instead, questions of human autonomy demand a vital engagement with reality that can borrow very little from any scientific conception of man. This will continue to be a central problem for the future of liberty and individual autonomy, especially in terms of the rapid rate of change in technological societies. Western societies have seen an increasing cry for anti-humanism that is often presented in the guise of a hyper-democracy.

Again, I must stress that my main concern — that is, my ultimately vital problem — addresses the question of my essence in the only way possible: as an entity of my own self-understanding. And only from the fruits of such a self-encounter can we create any greater cohesion between man and society. But, coming back to our critics... what can we say in good faith to those who do not seek genuine answers, but rather who make a sport of knocking about the sweat-drenched and will-testifying vital thought of others?

Philosophers for too long — I would argue, an incessantly long time — have wasted time and energy in trying to build collective castles and watering holes where all of mankind can go in order to rest and drink. This is particularly true of academic thinkers, and suggests reasons that may not be totally sincere in their foundation. I would strongly suggest that this is nothing other than a form of intellectual bloating. Philosophical reflection is a rigorous tool for ultimate human salvation, and not a social/political or even an epistemological aphrodisiac for the masses. The ultimate responsibility of the thinker lies in fashioning a reasonable degree of coherence to his existential perspective.[1] It is for this lack of a foolproof and closed-ended method that philosophy cannot be referred to as a science. Philosophy is neither a science or should it aspire to be. Regardless of this philosophy has been dealt a

63

debilitating card by people who insist that the role of the thinker is that of one who should concentrate merely on means of "commitment" to this popular theory, or that politically correct ideology. To pretend that the role of the thinker is that of public guru or minister of good works is to negate that philosophy is a manner of vital life that liberates us from objectification and that posits self-understanding as its own reward. Philosophical truths are not reached through committee. Today, a quick glance back at history can easily verify that all such attempts at creating a science of humanity have failed miserably.

We can easily prove this by going out into the daily world armed with the desire to understand; we quickly begin to see through the contradictions in the life of men — all men, like looking at the world through the holes in Swiss cheese. The true nature of human reality, then, appears to be fragmentation. And, what lies at the very core of this fragmented reality, or what Gabriel Marcel has called "the broken world"? The sensible answer to this is Man! Man is that destitute entity that always finds itself at the center of its own dissolution. The fact that reality is always terra incognita for man lies in the very make-up of human consciousness. But thought, much like human reality itself, is dialectical in nature and allows for a constructive and insightful search for the structure of our circumstances. The understanding that this is an inherent frailty in human reality allows for an honest foundation to all reflection. On the other hand, the failure to recognize this condition has often resulted in vicious crimes against the autonomy of the individual. This being the case, only mind can rectify this fragmentation and hence unify all subjective human experience into a cohesive unity.

---

1. Maugham seems correct in his sobering assessment that philosophers are responsible for offering "the plain man" a vision and suitable (even if tentative) answer to human concerns. He argues that to evade this aspect of the discipline is to neglect a central aspect of the philosophical vocation. He writes: "But the plain man's interest in philosophy is practical. He wants to know what is the value of life, how he should live and what sense he can ascribe to the universe. When philosophers stand back and refuse to give even tentative answers to these questions they shirk their responsibilities." See: *The Summing Up*, p. 261.

Of course, there is no guarantee that this cohesion, which mind works to attain, must always necessarily coincide with any morally viable or pleasant vision of a personal transcendence.

Individual perspectives will seek vastly different insights from the various faces that reality shows us. However, what best characterizes autonomy is the attempt to seek a central perspective that enables the reflective thinker to fuse together the understanding necessary to establish a dynamic and free-flowing subjectivity.

When we step out of our front door we can play a mental game where we ask ourselves: "How many people are genuinely in control of their lives, and how many have given this control over to external powers?" There is nothing obvious or certain about this question, but the answer seems clear given the auto-destructiveness of so many lives today. What else, then, is the discipline of philosophy for if not to address these questions and set human existence on firm footing? It seems to me that after twenty-five hundred years of philosophizing and twice that of mythology and religion, and another five hundred years of hard science, the human race should have a definite answer as to the true essence of man. But, this illusion is quickly frustrated after our initial encounter with the world, if not with existential reality altogether. It is not that man lacks a nature, necessarily, but rather that perhaps human essence is translucent. The solutions to existential concerns are never offered ready made. For this reason, we can come to the life-affirming and thus life-saving conviction that all meaningful attempts at philosophical reflection ought to be geared to questions of individual autonomy.

Perhaps adding fuel to the apparent confusion of the status quo of philosophical reflection is the artificial divide that academic philosophers have created between philosophy as a way of life — that is, as an utterly necessary manner of bringing ourselves out of a dark woods, and philosophy as "theory." The inherent cynicism that lies at the forefront of materialist conceptions of man has, since the time of Pyrrho of Elis and the ancient cynics created a poisoned atmosphere where philosophies of life are downplayed. Today post-modernity attacks questions of personal meaning or significance as sophisms that are best abandoned altogether. But this positivistic arrogance and narrow vision ignores the very fact that it is precisely in the form of existential questions where true meaning resides. Instead, the great error of post-modernity is to detract meaning from individual autonomy by substituting this with alliance to collective structures. Today this utilitarian and historicist denial of any genuinely differentiated transcendence occupies the center of debates on what it means to be human. Thus, we have witnessed an inordinate and disproportionate degree of attention paid by professional philosophers, that is, by teachers of the history of philosophy to the importance of collectively organized reality. The cost of this intellectual myopia to man's well-being has been devastating in terms of citing importance to human life solely as a utilitarian means to an end. This denial of personal transcendence, of course, has opened a flood of charlatanism from within as well as from outside the academy. Where the origin and proper role of philosophy have historically been to enlighten man by piecing together a coherent humanistic vision of man in the cosmos, today academic thinkers have instead converted her into a scholastic, theoretical prostitute. This merely anecdotal, self-referential, and self-contained effacing vision for philosophy serves no one well. Self-consuming word play is a perversion of philosophical vocation. On one hand, we can say that this kind of excessive intellectual hermitage destroys the inherent wealth that philosophy has offered to humanism. This degenerate anti-humanism continues to erode the vitality of life today. Viewed from the outside, the dearth of philosophical coherence has allowed for an explosion in the deformation of thought and the rigors that this responsible activity entails.

It must also be added that the respective vocations of thinker and scholar are not one and the same thing. Currently there seems to be great confusion on this point. Thus, if due to either vocation or necessity, as the case may be, we are called to be scholars, then we should see to it that we concentrate on pure scholarship. But the fundamental differences between these two poles have been blurred for far too long. Perhaps part of this has to do with the exigencies of the market place, the nature of university life or the demands of publishing houses. Perhaps. This has allowed for a serious confusion to arise as to the true purpose and need for philosophical thought. However, if our concern is one of an existential and vital necessity and not a scholastic luxury, we quickly arrive at the understanding that we must take our life into our own hands. But to achieve the latter possibility we must first comprehend that to succeed in this existential task it is also necessary to rely on our on convictions. Furthermore, this confusion has allowed, on the one hand, for the entrenching impression dating back to Auguste Comte that philosophy is a mere social-political activity. It has also enabled "gurus" of all kinds and denominations to pretend that they are "doing philosophy" just because they throw around some occasional philosophical terms.[1]

The Russian thinker Vladimir Solovyov communicates this same sentiment when he argues that all philosophy is best conceived and characterized as a tool for self-understanding or what amounts to salvation. And how many thinkers since Socrates and his favorite pupil, Plato, have stood atop a mountain peak and gazed down onto the world of men to find out that only an abyss could be seen from such heights? Hence Socrates' turn inward into questions of *eudaimonia* or the ancient notion of happiness is a life-saving vital move and not a form of intellectual gymnastics. This is exactly the raw awe that is felt by thinkers whose sole desire is to construct a unified worldview that allows for the existence of the individual in the universe. Socrates' notion that philosophy is simply a tool for the

---

1. Ortega y Gasset's insightful work *Ideas and Beliefs* (*Ideas y Creencias*) serves as a fine reminder of the interplay that exists between ideas and belies. Ortega does not argue that beliefs must be argued for or justified. Instead, he views beliefs as spontaneous and as necessary to serve the daily needs of man. Ideas, on the other hand are calculated and are always things that we "possess" whereas beliefs are more representative of "what we are." Beliefs embody us.

anticipation of death is an appropriate example of the form of reflection that is suited for the understanding that time and subjectivity can never be separated.

It is said that philosophy is born of wonder and awe. We can say with great certainty that this awe is a confrontation with the ethos that intuits the sublime nature of human reality. From this initial clash with a brazen and discriminating reality the individual is moved to find a place for himself in this seemingly overwhelming totality. However, economy of expression becomes essential to this self-reflective process, as empty and chic sophisms only give rise to world-weariness and cynicism.

There is a long and fruitful philosophical tradition of attempting to decipher the meaning and complexity of human affairs in what amounts to a neatly cropped and self-explanatory statement: the maxim.[1] Maxims have always served as direct, compact and insightful remainders that the problems of human existence can only be solved or at least addressed with a brand of moral courage that is absent from other aspects of thought which are offered for mass consumption. The lasting value of the maxim as a philosophical form is perhaps its inherently spontaneous quality. While theory surges forth from a calculative and not a spontaneous

---

1. The philosophical insight that maxims offer have always conveyed the kind of vital and life-grounding "truths" that people of all levels of culture and education can abide by. Maugham's perceptive work, *The Summing Up* is in my opinion one of the greatest source of philosophical, artistic, and literary criticism ever written. I will argue that this is the case because this is a kind of intellectual and vital autobiography that attempts to situate the life and meaning of one individual in objective reality. Beginning with section IXIV, he attempts to keep the myopia of academic philosophers from becoming full-blown blindness. He writes: "There is no reason why philosophers should not be also men of letters. But to write well does not come by instinct; it is an art that demands arduous study. The philosopher does not speak only to other philosophers and to undergraduates working for a degree, he speaks also to the men of letters, politicians and reflective persons who directly mould the ideas of the coming generation. They, naturally enough, are taken by a philosophy that is striking and not too difficultly assimilated. We all know how the philosophy of Nietzsche has affected some parts of the world and few would assert that its influence has been other than disastrous. It has prevailed, not by such profundity of thought as it may have, but by a vivid style and an effective form. The philosopher who will not take the trouble to make himself clear shows only that he thinks his thought of no more than academic value." p. 242.

operative mode, maxims, on the other hand arise out of an essential necessity and the indispensable desire to understand a particular situation. Even though the truth that maxims convey can seem unsystematic and in somewhat of a piecemeal fashion they are nonetheless always vital in scope. Maxims are quick to uncover and cite the essences that adhere between the spatial and temporal fabric of human reality. For this very reason the thinker that chooses to voice his understanding in this manner often strikes an essential cord in human existence, which if one takes the necessary care to comprehend can be very enlightening.

The maxim is to adults what the fable is to the child. The essence of both is that there is always a moral to be drawn. Of course, part of the problem that some thinkers have in accepting the truth and wisdom of maxims is precisely because in this day and age, the unifying notion of truth that maxims exalt is denied equal footing with the many fashionable theories that seek the light of day. The epistemological fragmentation that twentieth-century nihilism has brought about has all but obliterated any concern or respect for universal truth. The essence of the maxim is to make sense of the "uninstitutionalized" truths that are nevertheless contained within the metaphysical structure of human existence.

The central role and importance of maxims to the discipline of philosophy can neither be undermined nor denied, even in this positivistic and caustic age. Beginning with the ancient Greeks, and rapidly spreading through Roman schools of philosophy, maxims have attempted to organize the splintered nature of human reality. This scattered and untidy reality need not be viewed as a negative thing. But because the world of human experience is presented to us in pieces, that is, snippets of reality, at any given time, our understanding must attempt to compensate by unifying reality into a cohesive experiential field. The intent of the maxim is to fill in the spaces where truth serves as a corrective measure where common sense is missing.

Marcus Aurelius and Epictetus both illustrate this point. It cannot go unnoticed as an ironic historical fact that Epictetus — the slave — was to become teacher of the Roman Emperor, Marcus Aurelius, in the latter's youth. The maxim works as a raw mirror to the human will, where institutions, religion or the state are not made responsible for man's problems. Epictetus makes the following observation in his *Discourses:*

> Where lies good? In the will. Where evil? In the will. Where lies that which is neither good nor evil? In things inevitable.[1]

The maxim has the disquieting, and for some, the burdensome effect of positing man's existence as a cosmic being, and not as a political animal, as we have become so accustomed to think in the modern world. Perhaps few in an imprudent age will find this timeless moral instruction worth a second look, but this does not invalidate the truths and drama of human reality that Epictetus, for instance, alludes to in all his counsels. Epictetus can teach us that the real import of moral duty is the demands that this places on itself, unlike faceless and often empty categorical imperatives. A clear message of all maxims is the necessity for a vital philosophical understanding that acts to bind the thinker to the objective world. In man's quest for inner tranquility Maxims make very few demands of the external order, but rather on man himself.

In addition to this ancient sense of resignation, one can also point out the sovereign respect that Boethius shows for philosophy when this Byzantine thinker calls her a lady in his masterful work *Consolation of Philosophy (De Consolatione Philosophiae)*. Boethius was a worldly man who served Theodoric, the king of the Ostrogoths, and who was eventually executed for high treason. The striking thing about this work is that it is a dialogue between the thinker and philosophy or what amounts to a reflective monologue. Boethius asks Philosophy, whom he calls a grand lady, to tell him where happiness lies; she responds that it is not to be found in anything of this world. Thus a person like Boethius in the end must console

---

1. Epictetus: *Discourses* and *Enchiridon*. Translated by Thomas Wentworth Higginson. Roslyn, N.Y.: Walter J. Black, Inc., 1944. p. 127.

himself with that entity with whom he is in greatest agreement: himself.

More recent examples of this vital need for philosophical reflection can be found in *The Art of Worldly Wisdom*, a book of the fifteenth-century Spanish Jesuit Baltasar Gracian. Gracian's moral stoicism is said to have influenced both Nietzsche, who refers to him as the finest example of European moral subtlety, and Schopenhauer, who calls Gracian's book a companion for life. Gracian's emphasis is on the avoidance of folly through the exercise of prudence. Prudence in many ways is already a form of self-knowledge. Gracian's thought encompasses great respect for the moral life, but it does so with the understanding that rigid moral codes cannot embrace all of man's circumstances. Instead, Gracian promotes a form of self-knowledge that is open to adapting to different circumstances.

The traditional appeal of maxims has been mainly to embrace the philosophical desire for sincerity. Moreover, we must add that it appears that maxims, with their economy of words and endless use of ellipses in the service of brevity, reflect a central theme that has to do with the lack of tolerance for dishonesty and insincerity. Undeniably, these themes serve as a profound boost to this genre, given today's level of cynicism that is made worse by the ever-present clamor of the written word. The maxim's central truth is conveyed in the hope that the reader will agree that truth must not become overwrought with what is often ostentatious and detached technical jargon. It is traditionally assumed by writers of maxims that what is genuinely true can be stated clearly, succinctly, and without pomposity. In addition, the writer of maxims understands that time is the irrefutable test of truth. Traditionally, people with little or no formal education have understood the inherent meaning of maxims. What, after all, ought to be the aim of stating the truth if it cannot be communicated as such?

La Rochefoucauld's maxims also demonstrate a clearly articulated desire to showcase the follies of human nature by paying attention to one individual at a time. But more so, maxims are snapshots of the essences that man is blind to, but that eventually make us pay for our ignorance in matters of prudence. In this respect we can also point out that the thought of La Rochefoucauld played a profound influence in the maxims of both Chamfort and Voltaire. While maxims force us to look at our own improprieties, few people ever do so because of the misguided impression that maxims speak of entire classes and certainly not of individuals. For some people the message of maxims is lost in the comfort of anonymity. Part of the reason for this also has to do with the translucent nature of consciousness. The strength of maxims is that they challenge us to become aware of this ephemeral condition of human existence. This is perhaps the ultimate irony contained in maxims. When La Rochefoucauld writes, "Neither the sun nor death can be looked at steadily," the implication seems to be that to suffer from too much truth is as bad as ignoring truth altogether. This anticipates Nietzsche's contention that truth is best captured when embraced with a glance and not directly. However, the wisdom in this statement is found in the fact that by the time we come to apprehend this truth on our own, we already possess it. We can also add that the truth that maxims attempt to illustrate can only be grasped through a solitary sojourn. Unfortunately, truth is often watered down or prostituted in wider circles, where essentially it ends up not addressing anyone in particular. The nature and purpose of maxims seems best suited for the subjective, individual reality that reaches out to embrace it. But in manners of understanding, an ancient rule of thumb is that we come to understand what we are privy to given our own inherent constitution. For instance, some have criticized existentialism's lack of system-like qualities as being more like a mood and less of a philosophy. But this is to ignore the fact that, like existentialism, maxims too speak of human existence as a differentiated, personal and subjective fact. This fact can never be ignored. For this reason maxims can never attain the status of ideology. While ideology serves as a central rallying point through which life is viewed, maxims have no such collective illusions. Maxims originate from the presupposition that each individual must confront life on his own terms. For this reason maxims only convey a level of truth that is proportionate to our level of engagement.

Of course, any time one speaks of the truth that is conveyed through maxims the work of Arthur Schopenhauer must be mentioned. Schopenhauer — a thinker who often appears to be the whipping boy for the outwardly philanthropic, is a central figure in the modern use of the maxim. His main problem, I would argue, is that he paid too much attention to Hegel and the academic world of his time. Schopenhauer's lasting legacy might be his conviction that Hegel ushered in the age of intellectual dishonesty through his insistence that man's historical mission was the dwarfing of the individual by the forces of history. Schopenhauer is best known by his metaphysical masterpiece, *The World as Will and Idea*, but his works *The Wisdom of Life* and *Counsels and Maxims* recall a time when philosophical thought was hinged on the value of eternal and universal questions that pertain to vital human existence. These two works are interesting in their own right precisely because they do not speak of philosophical systems, but of individuals. Schopenhauer admits that the central tenet of his systematic work, *The World as Will and Idea* is not exactly a self-congratulatory vision of human fate. However, his two works of maxims do leave the reader with the marked impression that existence, with all of its disappointments and suffering, is a higher value than non-being. Schopenhauer's thought ministers to the leveling of pretense in human existence. What greater pleasure than to unmask hypocrisy? This much he can be said to have achieved. His thought on the nature of happiness, for instance, originates from the notion that our internal constitution contributes more to our well being than our possessions or our social standing. This is why Schopenhauer attributes such great importance to solitude. Solitude, he argues, works as a mirror to our personal make-up. On the other hand, the avoidance of solitude is the admission of an existential void. When he assures the reader that a high degree of intelligence often leads to a low level of passion and strength of will, he is arguing from a conviction that notices a natural system of checks and balances in human life.

And what can we say about the ardent individualist that is Miguel de Unamuno? Where do we rank that irreverent Spanish Gardener? Unamuno viewed systematic and academic thought as imperious, as deriving its power from making man turn his back on himself. Unamuno's philosophy is disseminated throughout his books of essays, novels, plays and poetry. Once, while gardening, Don Miguel was confronted by his neighbor who, walking by, asked him if he did not mind working so hard. Don Miguel was sweaty, muddy and hot. Unamuno, in his usual stoic manner, simply answered "no." The next day Unamuno was writing down some personal reflections in his study, with his window wide open; the same neighbor walked by. Unamuno caught his attention by saying, "You see, now, *this* is work." Unamuno's entire work is a meditation on the nature of human mortality and the quiet, stoic heroism that man must endure. Personal existence for Unamuno represents a constant struggle for autonomy.

And where do we place the morally courageous Albert Camus in the history of the maxim? Where can we place such a solitary figure in the history of philosophy? Camus is a fine example of the thinker as prolific writer. The importance of his thought is magnified by the fact that Camus wrote and thought in an age when the value of philosophy was increasingly being tied to academic philosophy. The fact that he wrote essays, novels, and plays attests to the fact that the main concern of the thinker is always one of self-understanding. The genres that thinkers use to develop their thought ought to be secondary to the reflective act itself. The philosophically mature Camus balked at the sight of collective renditions of human existence. But for this independence of thought he paid a heavy personal price.

Often, a concrete example of the regard that some thinkers have for subjectivity is manifested as a vital reflection on the passage of time. At the age of twenty-five, when Camus wrote his first novel, *A Happy Death,* his sole preoccupation was with the question of time.

74

Apparently Camus' manner of embracing life seems inimical for some critics. What most people consider to be depressing or nihilistic in Camus' work is his refusal to accept the terms that death places on conscious and self-reflective beings. For this reason we see the young Camus already embarking on the understanding of themes that are very concrete and which have everything to do with personal subjectivity. He writes, in *A Happy Death*:

> But if it was to do so, he realized that he must come to terms with time, that to have time was at once the most magnificent and the most dangerous of experiments. Idleness is fatal only to the mediocre. Most men cannot even prove they are not mediocre.[1]

Camus' grasp of time and his acceptance of destiny are similar to Kierkegaard's idea of the stages of life. Man's existential maturity, he argues, does not come about automatically but rather as the result of reflection. His understanding of the vital union that exists between life and time is clearly indicated by the central themes in *A Happy Death*. Camus' work places a high value on man's existential understanding of time and how this reality lies at the center of what it means to be human. Mediocrity for him is a state of existence where man negates his essence and lives from day to day like an existential vagrant. Similarly, this idea of mediocrity can also be found at the heart of Ortega y Gasset's notion of inauthenticity. One curious fact to be observed in Camus' thought is his lack of reliance on technical terminology or neologisms. Camus' conception of life is always that which is intuited, lived as reality and thus felt. But this activity, we must reiterate, is precisely what philosophy has always entailed. One can argue that Camus' thought is an example of finding the appropriate inferences that best establish the relationship between philosophy and life. If living time's immediacy and later retelling it is what vital philosophy is, then, this same manner of doing philosophy is precisely what Husserl's entire philosophical project entails. As such, Camus has very little need of

---

1. Camus, Albert. *A Happy Death.* Translated by Richard Howard. New York : Alfred A. Knopf, 1961, p.82.

systematizing his thought into something that would go against the grain of what is lived or felt.

And what about Luis-Ferdinand Celine's courageous and solitary use of personal freedom? What is his legacy in regards to any understanding of subjectivity and individuality in the twentieth century? Celine is the independent thinker par excellence, a thinker with unrestrained effusions and a fascination for the unfinished sentence. Somewhat dramatic at times, his greatest contribution to thought is that writing is as much about what we leave out as the sentences that we weave together. Taken as a whole, Celine's outbursts seem to suggest that man's explicitly expressed contradictions are unified at a much deeper and latent level. Celine attempts to cut through the veil of deception, duplicity, and hypocrisy that only serve to complicate human existence. His is not abstracted or theoretical courage, but rather courage that is manifested in the flesh. What genuine emotions must be seething deep within a man to make him utter in *Castle to Castle*, "Anything goes, and you can do what you please as long as you're a fully recognized clown...you don't? That's too bad! No tent? The ax..."[1] Celine is here referring to what in many countries can be called the "godfather principle" or what amounts to "show me who you know and I will tell you how far you will go." His work is possibly one of the finest examples of subjectivist realism unveiled to date.

The visionary Polish writer Stanislaw Witkiewicz, too, proves in his exemplary novel *Insatiability* (1927) that the "murti-bing" pill is man's eternal and utopian aspiration and not necessarily the attainment of personal autonomy. The murti-bing pill was to be the cure-all, feel-good answer to the existential indignities that man has always had to endure. The role of this tranquilizer was to efface our worries and liberate us from existential turmoil. While human autonomy is a perpetually difficult process of self-understanding, the murti-bing pill has the effect of immediately settling the fears

---

1. Celine, Louis-Ferdinand. *Castle to Castle*. Translated by Ralph Mannheim. New York: Delacorte Press, 1968, p.

and anxieties of a materialistic and technological age. In *Insatiability*, Witkiewicz (who was also a philosopher, playwright and painter) anticipates the totalitarian reality of Eastern Europe in the 1930s. Witkiewicz rejected the demands made on the individual by what he considered to be a future totalitarianism molded by a bureaucratically forced egalitarianism. But, what exactly has changed in terms of man's existential concerns since that poor soul took his own life in 1939, preferring death to a socialist utopia? A close look at the experiences of recent decades would confirm that perhaps nothing, in fact, has changed. The central role of history is to demonstrate that time is the ally of true genius!

But if time is a filter that brings to the fore the value of thought and what has been written, suggested, and forced upon man by motives that are often more forceful than the mere love of truth, what does time leave out? I would argue that the history of the maxim as a vital and genuine form of human communication has the right intent in addressing the common threads in human existence. If one pays close attention to the concerns of philosophers throughout time, the evidence seems to demonstrate an overwhelming and very much disproportionate attention to matters of man as a collective entity, the sphere of social-politico-economic organization, matters of a scientific orientation and concerns for the overall nature of thought, language, and consciousness. But everywhere we find a dearth of concentration on questions of what it means to be an individual. I suspect that some of the reasons for this collective and impersonal mania for proof have to do with a desire to find patterns in all things human. But also important, I will argue, is the sheer boredom that overcomes some thinkers when dealing with matters of an autobiographical nature. Evidently, some people find more control over abstract theorizing than the rigors of existential existence. Even further still, I would suggest that placing man in a collective box is easier, more economical and perhaps more expedient a solution to human concerns than dealing with individuals as differentiated phenomena: as subjective entities. Regrettably, most of these expedient solutions take on an undeniably political and collective face that from the start are tainted with ideology at the service of power more so than for respect for human autonomy. Another reason that we can point out has to do with the psychological desire that most people have to belong to a greater clan in order to assuage the seemingly endless blows of life itself.

This question is interesting because the ever-present collectivist dream of utopia for the most part seems to best manifest itself in the realm of the social-political, whereas the individualist, subjectivist pole, let us call it, by its very nature is better suited to the philosophical/literary. These two realms do not have to be mutually exclusive by any means, of course. But when we begin to reflect on questions of temperament and personal autonomy we quickly begin to realize that the subjective impetus is a powerful and undeniable aspect of human reality.

In Sumerian wisdom literature, *The Epic of Gilgamesh* shows Gilgamesh taking on the powers of life and death as he scours the world searching for immortality after his young friend Enkidu has died. Surprisingly enough he takes his fight to a higher court of appeals than that which his elders can offer him. Like Camus' concern in *The Myth of Sisyphus*, this silent inward cry is always directed at life itself. Neither of these authors directs his scorn at political power or institutions that in the final analysis cannot contribute to man's search for existential contentment, if not happiness altogether. Apparently this is not enough for the ideologically malcontent.

Socrates, too, is a central figure in this attempt to ground all understanding in what is essentially knowledge of oneself or auto-gnosis. After having paid close attention to the works of thinkers that came before him (the pre-Socratics), Socrates turns his attention to the conviction that the only thing worth knowing is that which has to do with knowledge of oneself. His concern is not with a skeptical notion concerning the impossibility of knowledge, but rather with the wisdom that the highest kind of knowledge is vital knowledge of oneself. Armed with the conviction that concern for his existential condition should illuminate all other aspects of his life, Socrates comes to the realization that only then can he become morally productive in the world-at-large. Some of the pre-Socratics, whose main appeal had to do with questions that took their overall cue from the natural elements, offered a vision of human life that culminated in an early form of materialism. Socrates, noticing that this was an epistemological dead end reacted by demonstrating that the highest human value was the pursuit of a rational life. This was best manifested in the moral life of man. Thus Socrates' aphorisms, "Know Thyself" and "The unexamined life is not worth living," would prove to be more than the fancy of someone overwrought with subjectivism. Incidentally, the ancient Chinese philosopher Confucius, a thinker who was born about eighty years prior to Socrates, would observe that man, who is a greater reality than the state, should enlighten the latter with good will. Both thinkers showcase a form of moral humanism of the highest degree.

From the earliest of times the main concern of thinkers and writers demonstrates a desire to communicate and articulate a vision of what it means to be an individual. But, this same subjective concern, I will argue is also felt by many people who cannot voice their internal convictions with such ease. Is this perhaps why we have witnessed such elaborate social/political totalitarian systems and their nihilistic and destructive effects in the twentieth century? Suffice it to say that it is evident that such social-political monstrosities do not spring from a deep respect for the autonomous individual.

The importance of the maxim as a viable philosophical/literary form is best embraced if we realize that this form can make its appearance in diverse genres. Baudelaire's *Paris Spleen* is another fine example of this. Baudelaire called this work a lyrical impulse of the soul. His main point of departure in this manner of writing was to seek a style flexible enough to say that which a great many other styles/genres could not contain. *Paris Spleen* can be considered a collection of literary shorts, prose poems or even literary sketches, but the thoughts contained in this work are the true showcase of the book. The singular punch of the maxim is felt throughout this work as a sort of elegant rumination on the nature of naked human experience. Let us take his essay titled "Crowds," where he proposes that the notion of multitude and solitude can in fact turn out to be dual aspects of the same thing. His point is that the poet ought to "people his solitude" in order to learn to be alone in the crowd.[1] The maxim, thus, can be found imbedded in dialogue, poetry or in narrative, but the truths that it attempts to point out are often missed because they are not sought. Often, such truths are passed off as the whim of some colorful character. This point is best alluded to in the coda to *Fahrenheit 451* where Bradbury cites Laurence Sterne's conviction that digressions in literature account for the life and soul of reading. Sterne's clear implication being that literature cannot function without calling attention to diverse aspects of human experience in one way or other.

Another indication of the role of the maxim in human life is exemplified in Jean Cocteau's variably acerbic and caustic book of essays titled *Diary of an Unknown*, where his main train of thought is to put his life in historical perspective. The book was written in the last decade of Cocteau's life. Of all the topics that he writes in this illustrious work, the notion of the dialectical and thus latently contradictory nature of man takes center stage. Cocteau muses on the fact that no matter how well known and objective a truth may be its very central core message is always missed due to its newness. Does this then mean that perhaps truth is only understood in retrospect? Let us consider his insightful essay, "On the Preeminence of Fables," where he calls attention to the unsightly fact that truth has variables that few recognize once that we are caught in its mist. The effect of all this, Cocteau argues is the construction of the fable. Equally fecund is his essay "On Distances," where he observes that what makes us human always remains more

---

1. Baudelaire, Charles. *Paris Spleen*. Translated from the French by Louse Varese. New York: New Directions Books, 1970.

distant to us than the farthest observable galaxy. Cocteau's writing transcends classification, if only in his disregard for being pigeonholed as a thinker.

The encounter with our subjective existence always comes about as the result of a timely reflection on the essence of human existence and how this is manifested in "my life." But this is more like a vital-existential activity at times than it is an overtly rational process. Such vital activity may be deemed a form of auto-gnosis, but to know oneself does not necessarily prove that one has arrived at the nature of subjectivity, only at the necessary pre-condition for its attainment.

In concluding, I will argue that any time that we talk about individual autonomy mention must always be made of a great twentieth century thinker whose writing is a tribute to the insightful majesty of the maxim. E.M. Cioran was a Romanian thinker who called Paris home for most of his life. Amongst Cioran's best-known works are *The Trouble with Being Born* and *A Short History of Decay*. Cioran's thought cuts a deep swath through all forms of human folly and pretense. His stoicism is like no other found in the annals of twentieth-century philosophy. If only one theme of his thought is pointed out, then let this be that to attain full understanding and command of one's life as a subjective cosmic phenomenon comes with a price that few are willing to pay. Is this perhaps what Cioran means when he writes that to live is to lose ground?

CHAPTER 4. ON MEANING IN HUMAN EXISTENCE

> Man can do nothing but guess right and choose well,
> for he stakes his life in each decision, on every choice.
> This is why life is drama...what obscures this reality is
> that man risks his life in bits and pieces, he goes along
> risking fragments of his life; but since each of these is
> irreplaceable, the loss of life in them is less real.
> — Julian Marias

When Robinson Crusoe was shipwrecked he brought the values of the civilized world along with him. His solitary companions were his hopes and aspirations, his humanity and his civility. This inner reservoir proved invaluable in his quest for survival. In essence, it can be argued that Defoe's masterful work is a study in existential meaning. What can harbor a stronger regard for meaning in human existence than the mere act of survival? If we consider that Crusoe's entire world collapsed, leaving him with only his conscious, emotive, and volitional stock to spring meaning into his new life, we can then begin to view this classic work as a case study in meaning and purpose in human existence. Perhaps only a few other examples of such pronounced individual autonomy can be found in literature, Hamlet quickly comes to mind, and Don Quixote's metaphysical pursuits being another fine example.

Robinson Crusoe is Defoe's fictional account of a man named Alexander Selkirk who allegedly spent five years marooned alone on Juan Fernandez Island, off the coast of Chile. After his return to England, Mr. Selkirk's ordeal apparently did not make a great deal of commotion until Defoe took the man's story and converted it into a fictional adventure tale. This true story of human ingenuity and survival is interesting on several counts. First, it is important to realize that the heroism that Selkirk exhibited in his efforts to remain alive is probably no different than other forms of heroism that man exhibits in daily life. However, his isolation and physical environment exacerbated his desire to triumph over his circumstances, circumstances that took on epic proportions, where a human being struggles to overcome odds that are disproportionate to his natural ability. But the important aspect of his ordeal is not found in the literal details of his account but rather as an example of the degree of engagement with reality that human essence can achieve. Both tales, Selkirk's survival story as well as Defoe's literary rendition, will serve us well in this respect.

Selkirk's battle is with reality itself, regardless of how much attention readers may pay to the adventure element of the story. Yet his story does not and probably could never attain the degree of popularity that it deserved until it became fictionalized. The apparent irony and what has been so endearing in Defoe's tale for most readers is not so much its moralizing and stoic courage, but rather the adventure that this tale conveys. But this fact need not surprise most people. This is a failure in the human imagination to distinguish between aspects of reality that are more differentiated by degree than by class. Action and the visual connotations of a work of art, for instance, will undoubtedly, in most cases gain more adherents than a character's inner drama.

It can also be argued that Robinson Crusoe is interesting because upon Mr. Selkirk's return to England he retained the very moral qualities that allowed him to survive his ordeal. The lack of interest that this man draws in his own right when stripped of his exciting adventure proves that what attracted most people to the story was its action component. This is a curious fact of human nature.

Robinson Crusoe has traditionally been recognized as a straightforward adventure story. However, on closer inspection the story also proves to be an engaging study in human character. The classical notion of character that the story entails is an attempt to look at the person in its totality. Character originates from a Greek word that is defined as the sum total of a person's traits. Character can also be explained as a unifying central core trait that guides a person's behavior, thoughts, and emotions. One can easily defend this view by understanding the degree to which moralizing plays a central role in Defoe's other works. This same moralizing can be found in Defoe's *Moll Flanders* and *Journal of the Plague Year*, as well. Another significant point is that *Robinson Crusoe* was written when Defoe, who was a worldly man by all accounts, was nearing sixty years of age. According to Defoe, Crusoe symbolizes the values of the self-reliant man par excellence. He is industrious and quick to adapt to such an alien environment. He is also resilient enough to restart his projects once that their practical utility has been exhausted and his hope has vanquished. Upon finding himself in this hostile environment, Crusoe comes to the realization that he is in danger. He says:

> In a word, I had nothing about me but a knife, a tobacco-pipe, and a little tobacco in a box. This was all my provision; and this threw me into such terrible agonies of mind, that, for a while, I ran about like a madman. [1]

But after he confronts this initial state of fear, Crusoe's ingenuity takes over. His resolve beckons him to survive his first night by sleeping embedded on the branches of a tree in order to avoid falling prey to any beast that may live on the island. In

---

1. Daniel Defoe. *Robinson Crusoe: Travels and Adventures*. The Spencer Press, 1937. p. 46.

addition to this safety measure he notices that there is a prickly kind of tree nearby that, if he is careful in climbing, will most likely equally ward off tree-climbing animals. He reasons:

> Night coming upon me, I began, with a heavy heart, to consider what would be my lot, if there were any ravenous beasts in that country, seeing at night they always come abroad for their prey. All the remedy that offered to my thoughts, at that time, was to get up into a thick, bushy tree, like a fir, but thorny, which grew near me, and where I resolved to sit all night, and consider the next day what death I should die, for as yet I saw no prospect of life. [1]

Robinson Crusoe is a story of the human will and its desire to triumph over objectifying material circumstances. Defoe, who was known to be a religious non-conformist, identified himself with the values of the working class. Robinson Crusoe's character reflects practicality, perseverance, and resolve in his actions. Eventually, after the initial fire of hope begins to fade his practical will leads him to make a permanent home on the island. Defoe takes the reader on an intimate trek of this man's emotions and thoughts. The story begs the discerning reader to ask, "What would I do under such circumstances?" The implication of this rhetorical question seems to be that Robinson Crusoe brought to the island the necessary moral character to survive. What does not seem to be the case is that Crusoe's resoluteness was something that he picked up all of a sudden.

Even his ability to deal with crushing disappointments tells the reader something substantial about this man's moral qualities. For instance, when Crusoe finished building a boat that has taken a long time to complete he becomes shocked to realize that the size and weight of the boat is too much for any one man alone to launch to sea. This is a devastating defeat to his hope of leaving the island, but his will quickly adjusts to this reality and rapidly turns to other endeavors.

---

1. Ibid., p. 46.

Of course, Crusoe's main preoccupation is in trying to stay alive and, progressively, to come to terms with the decreasing hope of ever leaving the island. This hope, regardless of its meagerness, brings meaning to all his actions. But meaning, as is also often the case with health, for instance, is one of those gray aspects of human life that most people do not bother with until these are depleted. Thus it is easy to see how meaning and significance are not sought out as ends in themselves. Instead, they are subsidiaries of hope. Personalists argue that persons are the supreme reality in the cosmos, and as such personality must be allowed to confront the objective order on its own terms. Crusoe's plight on the island is to take on the cosmos with what up to then was a civilized regard for autonomy, but that has now turned into his best tool for survival. Meaning, then, is often found in the situating of life whereby all the external forces that a subject encounters can be accounted for and embraced by personality. Regardless of all the other possible connotations that meaning may have for human beings, it remains to be said that it is always acts as a blanket of security.

Meaning and the significance that we attribute to different aspects of reality can never be separated from our personality. Undoubtedly meaning in human existence mandates that the personality of the subject coincide with the objective exigencies of its activity. A failure of this cooperation between subject and object does not necessarily negate meaning, for the subject must adapt to many extraneous situations, but it does force a necessary change of values. This initial state of disagreement can lead to disappointment, but this fluid aspect of reality is precisely what an intuitive personality learns to foreshadow. Ironically, this resistance to the inner strife of the subject is commensurate with the possibility for a meaningful existence.

But what exactly is meaning if not that which lies at the periphery of all human activity? Moreover, we cannot refer to meaning without taking purpose into consideration. These two questions are interrelated in such a way in human existence that it becomes difficult to make sense of meaningful events that lack purpose. It is easy to see this mutual dependency if we consider and remain consistent to the aforementioned condition that meaning is not necessarily consciously sought. Thus we can define purpose as: resoluteness, a desired outcome or the settling of a goal. While purpose can be attained without necessitating an overwhelming sense of meaning in human existence, meaning, on the other hand denotes a holistic and even a teleological fulfillment.

The animal world is a fine arena to showcase the inherent differences between these two notions. When a bird builds a nest it is clearly undertaking a purposeful process in terms of function. The bird's main and most likely only objective is to have a place to incubate its eggs. In cases when storms or other animals destroy the nest, birds can be seen busily and efficiently rebuilding the nest. The purpose of this activity is to build a nest regardless of any regard or allegiance to meaning. Similarly the purpose of having a queen bee in every hive signals the existence of a hierarchical organization that allows for the cultivation of honey. It is very unlikely that the question of meaning plays a part in this activity. Hence we can see that one of the characteristic differences between meaning and purpose has to do with the internal or subjective nature of meaning, whereas purpose may be met as an external or objective reality.

Likewise, let us ask what kind of entity can create seemingly endless life possibilities for itself? Human life, as far as we can tell, is the only cosmic phenomenon that places this burden on itself despite our often conscious or unconscious protestations. Thus human existence is a self-conscious and temporally driven form of life that seeks auto-understanding. From these temporal possibilities we encounter purpose or the lack thereof. From such possibilities we can also find a reference or what amounts to a designation from which we can anchor our notions of meaning. These questions are important to a being that spends its entire lifetime pondering over questions of its own design. Hence one might argue that all human construction is in one way or other an attempt to quench our need to engage in meaningful activity. However, as previously stated, this does not have to necessarily translate into a conscious effort. But the satisfaction humans receive from creating objects regardless of the emotional and vital scope of their aesthetic form is also an attempt to grapple with a rewarding sense of purpose. To leave something to posterity so that others may find their lives enriched by our work, if not also by our memory, brings a sense of fulfillment to our existence. This is one reason why we create museums, libraries, and other institutions that salvage and safeguard our collective history for posterity. This is also one of the main reasons that people give for collecting objects that in many instances only have a subjective meaning to the collector. Could this also be a reason why reading biographies and especially autobiographies is such a fulfilling form of reading for some people?

Even then, these are questions that, depending on our foundational presuppositions, may yield no apparent answers, only subjective reasons for their undertaking. Having said this, it is still highly conceivable that the hopes and aspirations that lead to meaning are nothing more than what in Descartes' day were considered chimeras. Can the search for meaning or engagement in such activities be a delusional cul-de-sac? This could very well be the case when considered from an "objective" viewpoint. But the problem is that few people have ever been able to retain such a viewpoint without paying an immense and life-negating prize. Also, to take this particular epistemological stance is to assume a radically detached and ultra-objective position that has never been a viable possibility for man. Part of the reason for this, I will argue, is that an entity that can ask such questions has no other recourse but to begin his questioning from a given presupposition. This is not only a necessary condition of human consciousness as we know it, but also an admission of the inherent limitations and constrains that such questions place on the person who poses them. It cannot be denied that the question of meaning in human existence showcases a marked practical value. Thus to maintain that meaning is a subjective phenomena inevitably proves to be self-contradictory because in posing the idea that all notions of meaning are pointlessly subjective, such an argument establishes itself as a further example of meaning. Hence, logically speaking, we cannot negate the alleged circularity of all arguments that attempt to establish the kingdom of meaning. This is not an instance of radical skepticism, but a manner of settling disputes that must be addressed by individual vital subjects. The question of meaning, then, has a practical and lived urgency, the value of which cannot be squandered on mere intellectual disputes.

What, then, is so important in this quest to enlighten human existence with some overarching and satisfying conscious rendition of a nature that is truly our calling? This search is important in that it can root our lives along the lines of a central, vital axiological axis. From a strictly practical point of view, our preoccupation with meaning proves to be the most human of enterprises. This endeavor is the strongest and most effective tool that we have in our disposition to combat the ravages of cynicism, world-weariness, and time.

We witness this sense of wonder in the fresh approach to life that is found in children, for instance. Children do not search for meaning. Instead they are simply fulfilled by the static uniformity that time exhibits for them. In the young this sense of wonder can dictate the future pathos of an emotionally well-balanced existence. But this same sense of wonder can refresh the perspective of the middle aged, especially after we have lost our way due to world-weariness. Despite the many trivialities of daily living, a fresh approach to old questions, events or situations opens up a new avenue of possibilities where previously none seem possible. The exercise of meaning is achieved through the grounding of vital beliefs, never by theory. This latent optimism is perhaps one of the greatest learning that adults can take from children. For instance, when Crusoe managed to successfully create an earthen pot in which to cook his meals, he could not contain his excitement. He writes:

> No joy at a thing of so mean a nature was ever equal to mine, when I found I had made an earthen pot that would bear the fire; and I had hardly patience to stay till they were cold, before I set

one on the fire again, with some water in it, to boil me some meat, which I did admirably well; and with a piece of a kid I made some very good broth, thought I wanted oatmeal and several other ingredients requisite to make it so good as I would have had it been.[1]

Crusoe's character is also an example of how surprisingly resilient human beings can be. Much like a child, he gains immeasurable joy from seemingly minor events. Seeing a man's footprint on the shore, under the circumstances, becomes a momentous event. This demonstrates that motivation or intent is in many instances more rewarding than their effects. Equally important, this quest motivates the old when faced with questions of an ultimate nature. In the old the glance of this quest is easily turned backwards to embrace the importance of memories, given the proximity of the inevitable mortality that is in fact our true destiny.

Miguel de Unamuno's sole philosophical concern was with the question of immortality.[2] Depending on how we attack such a concern, he reasoned, so will turn out to be the overall quality of our lives. We ought not to lose sight of the fact that merely asking such questions brings a sense of control to our lives that we would otherwise relegate to mere chance. The greatest understanding that comes from the thought of thinkers like Kierkegaard, Nietzsche, and Unamuno, for instance, is that to truly come to terms with the nature of reflection is always to find ourselves alone. These are thinkers for whom to philosophize meant to live. For them, philosophy turns out to be a guide map that allows us to unravel a direction to the course of our lives. And if for this reason alone philosophy must always show a subjective and personable face. But the nature of wonder or Philo-Sophia, the love of wisdom, as Socrates calls this task is always a solitary exercise in subjectivity.

---

1. Ibid., p.122.
2. See: Miguel de Unamuno. *Del Sentimiento Trágico de la Vida: En los Hombres y en los Pueblos.* Madrid: Editorial Plenitud, 1966. This work was translated into English in 1926 as *The Tragic Sense of Life in Men and in Peoples.*

From its earliest days in ancient Greece, to philosophize was never an intellectual sport, as is often the impression one receives today from reading scholastic "nay-sayers" whose sole concern is with criticism and the destruction of previous rational systems of inquiry. It goes without saying that sophists, in any age, have always had little regard for truth. To them the true point of rhetoric and to play devil's advocate, as the case may be, is to derail any attempt at establishing a philosophically sound ground for the good life. But this destructive activity is never an example of philosophy proper. The role of the philosopher is that of reconstructing the *kosmos* (world order) due to a pressing need to create a viable existential ground for itself. Introspective thought is the union of our vitality, or what amounts to our life force with our subjectivity.

Reflection is a tool that ought to be geared toward aiding the vitality that is differentiated conscious life. More so, reflection is an activity that serves as the basis of our salvation as temporal entities. Man cannot negate his inherent need to wonder. But equally true, our existential inquietude will determine our ability to make sense of reality and to find comfort and security in human existence. Also added to man's existential malaise is the temporal condition that does not allow the luxury of waiting to collect all of the available "evidence." Existential concerns force us to seek our understanding from whatever sources that may serve as anchors for our existence. These sources may originate with our intellect, will, emotions, and passions, and even with a keen "smell" for reality — that is, with an intuition for the order of things. What is not permitted is to place existential concerns under a microscope in the manner of physical objects. We do not enjoy the luxury and necessary objective distance from ourselves to dissect our lives into its appropriate micro components. To attempt to do so comes at the cost of neglecting the fulcrum of human existence: the subjective-I. To be awed by the splendor of human existence, with its eventual sorrow and misery, is a vocation that is not easily quenched through overly zealous epistemological proofs. Between the necessary call for objectivity that man demands of the other and the inner world of his own subjectivity, there exists an immense gulf that is more often than not the realm of the ineffable.[1]

What a ludicrous turn of events it was when the positivists asserted that a statement is meaningful, if and only if, it can be verified.[2] Nowhere in nature does life manifest itself in such conditional and anti-septic terms. The ultimate naïve arrogance comes when the Vienna Circle posited that metaphysical statements were equivocal. Even the positivistic Wittgenstein had to turn to the intuitive nature of the ineffable in order to retain some vital meaning to live his life by. He arrived at the conclusion that the real and lasting essence of the world is not to be found in the world, but beyond it.[3]

But how can anyone verify the joy that we get from holding our newborn child, walking our children to school, or being moved by a vitally uplifting idea? And why would anyone want to? And isn't this mania for theory, data, and objectivity in existential matters a sign of an insipidly entrenched and sophomoric thought? What must be the outward signs of joy or even simple contentment? Perhaps this is where the whole edifice of post-modernity has gone awry? Perhaps the greatest problems of post-modernity have something to do with this incessant desire to ground all forms of thought in centerless, formless external factors. The contradictions of post-modernity can no longer be contained by further "theorizing." The unceasing desire to do away with metaphysical concerns is probably the most inane of man's obsessions. There is no benefit to this spirited disregard for ultimate human questions besides those of building monolithic totalitarian panaceas. Some of

1. In his 1922 book, *The Great Secret*, the writer and 1911 Nobel-Prize winner Maurice Maeterlinck explores the varying conditions that give meaning to human life. The work attempts to fuse together knowledge from various traditional sources ranging from the physical sciences to the Kabbalah.

2. See: J. Bronowski. *Science and Human Values*. (Perennial Library; New York, Harper & Row, Publishers, 1965) p. 59.

3. See: William Barrett's book, *The Illusion of Technique: A Search for Meaning in a Technological Civilization*. Barrett is one of the best and most balanced expositors of existentialism. He argues that the later Wittgenstein embraces a more vital and existential approach to life due to a failure of positivism to ground itself in human existence.

these attacks on metaphysics have originated in an obstinate and misplaced respect for the scientific method. But philosophers must realize from the outset that the scientific method is not equipped to undertake questions that deal with the inner life of man. The repeated failure of attempts to ground the social sciences in the method of the hard sciences demonstrates this fact. The logic that animates human freedom and the psychic process that leads to this is an open-ended affair. As such, the dialectic that is at work in human existence is the culmination of will, reason, emotions, and passion. Unlike the nature of physical objects or laws, human existence does not exhibit a static level of predictability from which a sound science of man can be enacted. The fact that every thinker restructures the logos of the world ought to serve as a reminder that everyone who puts their nose to the grindstone of reality leaves their indelible mark on human affairs. The centralizing culmination of thought ought to be to seek equipoise between the objectifying nature of reality and the vulnerability of subjectivity. For this very reason William Barrett defends William James and existentialist thinkers in that they have attempted to philosophize in a personable and approachable manner. He writes:

> If philosophy is to say something that matters to us, it will have to touch upon the personal core of experience which after all is the center of being for all of us. And whatever else existentialism may have contributed by this time, I think it has at least succeeded in establishing some major reassessments in our judgments of past reputations: Kierkegaard and Nietzsche, for example, who philosophized in a most personal mode, now loom as two of the most powerful minds of the nineteenth century. We are less likely therefore to condemn William James out of hand for his personal style.[1]

I often witness more enlightenment and beauty in the logos of Platonism than I do in Comte's theology of "facts"; more truth in Aristotelian notions of individuality than in any Darwinian or materialist conception of a utopian collectivist anti-humanism;

---

1. Ibid., p. 280.

more sincerity in the playful paradoxes of Chesterton than in the sheer arrogance found in modern-day sophists.[1]

Is this search for the infinite, then — this infinite synthesis, as Immanuel Kant has so aptly called it, an inborn ability that is ingrained in our consciousness? That is, can this deep-rooted quest for the nature of the self be merely an epiphenomenon? If so, why then does the human brain suffer from this delusion? Or is this a concern that swells deep within the core of our self-conscious nature, one that perhaps establishes consciousness as a subjective rallying point for differentiation? It only seems prudent to answer this query by stating that if there is to be a central core to man, then we ought to look no further than to human consciousness. And is the structure of consciousness in man not so highly developed as to welcome answers to the questions that it poses for itself? If this is not possible, then we are still left to ponder the nature of this limiting masochism. Consciousness — as this is exhibited in human existence, again — I must de-emphasize mere biological life, is perhaps the logos and matrix of our salvation as well as the origin of our torment. The awareness of our subjectivity can serve as a fruitful foundation to all human endeavors, thus establishing the meaning of what a genuine humanism entails. To become aware of oneself creates a myriad of possibilities for such a being. But these vital possibilities along with the truths that it uncovers can confuse and

---

1. A close look at the acceptance speeches of the Nobel Prize in literature winners dating from 1901, the first year of the award, to the present demonstrates a formidable abundance of individuality that is clearly rooted in man's natural capacity for differentiation. A random selection of the ninety-nine winners (at the time of writing) clearly indicates the importance that traditionally writers have placed on subjectivity. From Miguel Angel Asturias (1967), who writes in his acceptance speech: "Thought unchained. Until arriving, once again, after the bloodiest verbal battles, at one's own expressions. There are no rules," to Albert Camus (1957), who writes: "Truth is mysterious, elusive, always to be conquered," all of these individuals in one way or other have elaborated on the nature of individuality and subjectivity. The extreme case of Jean-Paul Sartre (1964) and Boris Pasternak (1958), both of whom refused the prize, also alludes to the point that I am making. Sartre, while living in a free society, refused the prize because he believed that it would turn him into an "institution." Pasternak, on the other hand, who lived in the Soviet Union, was not only expelled from the Soviets Writers' Union but was also forced into not accepting the prize, as this would embarrass the totalitarian state.

frustrate a great number of people. This primal metaphysical freedom — let us call it by its name, can unfortunately become an asphyxiating burden for some people. Jean-Paul Sartre was correct in calling the problem of primal human freedom a true condemnation, one which most people exercise in bad faith. But bad faith is nothing other than knowing what we ought to do and yet not having the moral courage and will to enact it.

To reflect on the ontological nature of reality and to find ourselves located at the center of this vast cosmic conundrum is not only our true calling, but is also our salvation. Regardless of what we may find at the center of this maelstrom, some of us become dizzy with the taught that this unitary reality that we seek may just turn out to be our own life or whatever values this may engender. But regardless of our arrival at a successfully prescriptive answer, we nevertheless must attempt to transcend our itinerant and often all-too human perspective. Ironically, it is often the case that our perspective is too provincial when confronted with questions of meaning and purpose. This may seem like a paradox, given that the human perspective is one that we cannot escape given its finite possibilities. However, what conscious vision would demand of us that we side step our human circumstance for a possible glimpse into eternity or the void, as the case may be? The framework of our consciousness is flexible enough to permit such paradoxical nuances in our search for understanding. Let us call such a vision a split in consciousness, as it were. Our task, then, ought to be to try to view human existence as a truly cosmic phenomenon. This separation can enhance and amplify our vision of the human condition while also retaining a respect for subjectivity. We must also recognize that this kind of questioning already informs our possible answers. But the degree of success of such a task lies precisely in the very fact that the obvious is what we often miss the most. To be awed by the grandeur of space and time does not have to overwhelm us existentially This search for meaning always recoils back into our subjectivity.

We cannot deny that human existence is a solitary task. This, of course, does not entail that one must live in perpetual solitude. But even when surrounded by well-meaning, caring, and nurturing people we must nonetheless face our life from the inside out. That is, we must face our freedom and our circumstances with our personal vision and imagination. When lost in a dense forest we attempt to find our way out — human existence is no different. But because human existence is an existential solitary trek that we take through unknown, unsteady ground, as this often proves to be does not negate the possibility of finding a way out.

But truth, the very truth that allows for a good and contented life, is not necessarily relative, as this overly used word may suggest. The contention that is often made by critics is that these concerns of which we are now engaged in are nothing other than subjective claims. But to such sallow and unimaginative critics our immediate answer ought to be that human life is precisely this — a subjective phenomenon that attempts to make sense of itself by embracing the objective world. By this, then, I merely mean to state that we must all earn the right to possess meaning through our own effort. All cultural renditions of meaning, as pre-fabricated structures to which we can turn to receive comfort are admirable. But in essence no one can live our life for us.

In his surrealist painting, *The Promenades of Euclid*, René Magritte offers a vision of the world — of a reality that is at once magical, and fanciful, yet conceptually innovative. In this painting a wide boulevard whose lines are converging in the distance is flanked by a cone which makes up the top of a tower giving us a comparison between the sensual world and the conceptual or perceived reality of man. But as we take in the entire spectrum of the world seen through a window, we come to the understanding that the window, as well as the view of the city is a vista that is held up on a painter's easel. This painting allows us to see our everyday world in a refreshing manner by aesthetically removing us from our human condition. The same can be said of meaning in human existence as this unifying search allows us to fuse together fragments of reality that would otherwise never hold up under objective scrutiny. If it is true that perhaps truth is objective in nature, it is equally true that this truth can be attained through diverse perspectives. This may suggest that truth is splintered by subjectivity, but I would venture to argue that the role of reflection is precisely the opposite — that is, to assemble a mosaic through differentiation. Is this search for truth, then, also not a search for meaning, if only by implication?

In *Meditations on Hunting*, Ortega y Gasset offers a striking phenomenological stance of man vis-à-vis the kosmos. He argues that one of the most latent and descriptive renditions of the nature of man is our need for diversion. In diversion Ortega finds a roundabout manner of coming to terms with the passage of time and how this affects the fragile nature of our psyche. He elaborates:

> Yet serious examination should lead us to realize how distasteful existence in the universe must be for a creature — man, for example- who finds it essential to divert himself. To divert oneself is to separate oneself temporarily from what one usually is, to change for a while our usual personality for another which is more arbitrary, to attempt to escape for a moment from our real world to others which are not ours. Is this not strange? From what does man need to divert himself? with what does he succeed in diverting himself? [1]

Diversion for Ortega means the fulfilling of our lives. His notion of diversion cannot be separated from the human need for occupation. But for Ortega not just any notion of pre-occupation will suffice. The kind of occupation of our time — that is, of our lives that Ortega views as the most authentically human is an understanding of our vocation. Vocation, then, becomes for him the answer to the question of meaning.

He writes:

> When he becomes aware of existence, he finds himself before a terrifying emptiness. He does not know what to do; he himself

---

1. See: Ortega y Gasset's *Meditations on Hunting.* p. 19.

must invent his own tasks or occupations. If he could count on an infinity of time before him this would not matter very much: he could live doing whatever occurred to him, trying every imaginable occupation one after another. But — and this is the problem — life is brief and urgent; above all, it consists in rushing, and there is nothing for it but to choose one way of life to the exclusion of all others; to give up being one thing in order to be another; in short, to prefer some occupations to the rest. The very fact that our languages use the word "occupation" in this sense reveals that from ancient times, perhaps from the very beginning, has seen his life as a "space" of time, which his actions, like bodies of matter unable to penetrate one another, continue to fall.[1]

What makes Ortega's an existential analysis and not a political one, for instance, is his insistence that staying busy or becoming engrossed in praxis is not an authentic possibility for man. Instead, what gives man meaning is to find his vocation. The genuine driving force that allows man to situate himself in the great scheme of things is never found from without, but rather already as a constituent reality from within. This is why he goes on to say, "This strange phenomenon whereby we call on ourselves to do specific things is the "vocation."[2]

Equally true, the process of existence — or an existential existing, as the case may be, given that we always live the latter internally is an incomplete process. Karl Jaspers has referred to this truism as *mogliche existenz*. Jaspers' contention is that human existence finds itself to be incomplete because it is always becoming something other than what it is in its immediacy. This condition frustrates us due to our need for clarity and resolution. He argues that our work as existential subjects is to seek completion (das Umgreifende), in fact to transcend the fragmentary nature of human existence with a unifying picture of reality that he refers to as the comprehensive.

---

1. *Meditations on Hunting*, p. 23.
2. Ibid., p. 25.

We can only wonder as to how many people see their lives as a ready-made by-product of a bio-chemical process. My immediate impression is that a large percentage of people in a sterile technological age view their lives as ready-made or as a fixed existence. What I mean by this has everything to do with the lived emotion — the intuition some would add, that differentiated human life is an existential/aesthetic enterprise and never merely a material ready-made existence. It is difficult to counter this seemingly obvious reality with apparent scientific proofs, arguments and dehumanizing theories. After all, this assertion only addresses a fundamental truth of human existence. In a manner of speaking, we can say that only trees, dogs, and the fauna of the field are ready-made entities. By this I simply mean that they are entities that lack an internal dimension to their being. Due to this fact, their possibilities — or what amounts to their freedom is nullified. Paradoxically though, this is how some people today have come to view their lives. It seems rather strange and perplexing that such a self-conscious entity, as is man, should give away its freedom in exchange for an easy and apparent epistemological certainty. In other words, to believe oneself to be solely a biological entity, one whose very existential freedom relies on a neurological order seems like an easier road to take. This view promises greater existential levity, anyhow. Our freedom, that is, our free and consciously abiding choice to decipher our existence, as a conscious and dialectically lived process is what places us in a position to answer the ever present riddle, "what is man?" This, I believe to be true regardless of the professed findings of biological science. Any being that can ask this question and simultaneously posit an answer, I will argue, has already succeeded in extricating itself from the background noise of the material world. This fact, ironically, is already part of the seemingly objective scientific ethos.

This is perhaps a telling sign of the destructive and nihilistic nature of post-modernity — a spectacle is probably more accurate a description of this incessant attempt to negate thousands of years of civilization that have delivered us to this current self-conscious understanding of ourselves. This negation — this extirpation of our history is a paradoxical phenomenon, one that if we are not too pressed for time in our current quest for ideological obfuscation will soon fade away as an empty sophism. The vital toll that such nihilism takes on human lives, however, is another question altogether. This inflated and tortured post-modern consciousness that desires to negate man's spectrum of freedom can only be viewed as pathological.

So what then is the future of meaning and purpose in human existence? The question arises, I believe, quite legitimately due to our interminable desire to objectify and quantify all aspects of human existence. Invariably, this question, as is posed by post-modernity springs more from an apparent emptiness and not from a fullness of being. This raises a serious sign for concern. Ours can only be viewed as a morally and spiritually debased civilization in its insistence on fashioning all human questions in terms of a mechanistic "how?" What we often fail to recognize is that the nature of the question "how this...or that?" is only concerned with technical know-how, that is, only with the "how-of-things?" But only a culturally bankrupt epoch can ask questions with the apparent lack of existential zeal that we employ in this matter. Ortega was prophetic when he said that man gets used to living with decadence.

Part of the problem of our time is that materialism, in all its variegated forms excludes all other manifestations of human existence that cannot be verified. This crass and sophomoric attitude is what some argue for in the name of objectivity. Is not science a supreme testament to the being of man? Is this anti-humanistic nihilism the true and lasting legacy of materialism? We can refer to our age as being one where reason itself has been socialized. Ours is not a time of genius, but rather the opposite, a form of social, intellectual, and spiritual asphyxiation where thought is arrived at by committee. Today terrorism, in all its forms, seems to have finally found a "theoretical" foundation. It is perhaps a very telling sign of the times that our civilization should operate by the illusion that only through an artificially contrived mutual agreement can we even begin to answer what anything truly is or means. This is diametrically opposed to a time and age of true creative genius, when thinkers relied on their own vocation, experience, and ability in the creative process. We can probably conceive of a not too distant future when the great "nay saying" committees will only meet to affirm the fact that theirs is a lasting legacy that has been ingrained in our culture.

But people who are of good will (not a small feat, in itself) know — perhaps better yet, intuit, that meaning in our lives is felt from within, and is not arrived at through the inertia of external circumstances. Meaning, in human existence, is lived — not debated, or proven with mathematical equations, chemical tables, logical proofs or social-political ideology. Meaning, purpose, contentment, and wonder are fueled by the complexity, yet also the simplicity, of the apparent nature of things. I find it immensely amusing that when we are pressed to make sense of negative events and emotional fatigue in our lives, in times of crisis, for instance, none of our many fashionable theories seem to satisfy or ease our pain. Thus, it is fruitful to remember that the method of epistemology is best suited for scientific inquiry, and not for answering questions of an existential nature. "Theory," when viewed in terms of an existentially lived reality, comes across as a mere plaything. Dating back to the primal condition of mankind, we still do not possess a clear answer as to whether human consciousness can know the entire catalogue of the nature of reality. A greater question still, one that is perhaps not well suited for the coy and easily nauseated, is whether human beings really and truly care to know "the inner working" of all things? I wonder if in fact our epistemological uncertainties, in light of our mental deficiencies are not a natural response to an internal mechanism that is designed to help us fend off what Gabriel Marcel has called the "bite of reality." Thus, this is perhaps why we humans are always looking over our back, as it were, trying to figure out if our last move was the definitive one. Experience of the ineffable is never exhausted through epistemological proof. Epistemology is best equipped to tell us something about the physical world as matter, and not about the existential realm of human existence. There seems to be great confusion in this regard today. To experience the ineffable is to grapple with our own constitutive noetic structure. All of the great structures, super-structures, and institutions of man throughout the ages have attempted to answer this very same human riddle: what is man? These institutions, as is most visible in the case of myth, religion, and science are but a symbolic rendering of the make-up of reality in its totality. As fragments of a greater possible truth, these symbols are duly necessary, even though often limited in scope due to our human inadequacies and vision. When about 100,000 years ago Neanderthals — mere primitives by our standards — began to bury their dead, it can be argued that a subjective realization dawned within them. Their apparent decision not to abandon their dead any longer to the ravages of animals and climate was a move forward in the humanizing of our human condition. Equally true, the Egyptian preoccupation with the immortality of the soul leaves us with the impression that life, even with all of its misery, is still a treasure chest that we do not want to nor can we afford to close. Hence, to think that science or social-political ideology is the answer to all human metaphysical inquietudes is to walk a very fine tightrope between what there is and what we understand there to exist. This is the line between a healthy naiveté and a self-consuming arrogance.

J.B.S. Haldane, the British geneticist who along with Fisher and Wright is one of the founders of modern population genetic theory, makes this clear when he writes, "my own suspicion is that the universe is not only queerer than we suppose, but queerer than we can suppose."[1] These words conjure up the sound and fury of what we can label as a truly scientific and humanistic honesty.

---

1. Kenneth Clark. *Civilization: A Personal View.* (New York: Harper & Row Publishers, 1969. p. 345.

CHAPTER 5. LONELINESS AND IMMORTALITY IN ENRIQUE ANDERSON IMBERT'S "EL FANTASMA"

> Life is like crystal, the transparent medium through which we can see other objects. If we permit ourselves to be deluded by the strong desire that any transparent things implants in us, to pass heedlessly through it to something on the other side, we shall never see the crystal. — Ortega y Gasset

Enrique Anderson Imbert's provocative and engaging short story *El Fantasma* revolves around the death and subsequent unorthodox description of the afterlife by the protagonist. In Imbert's story the author compels the reflective reader to ask whether the existence of the soul, that is, of a conscious entity that retains its own identity after death, can exist. His answer to this question is a resounding yes! But quickly thereafter, the reader realizes that Imbert's main line of questioning has nothing to do with the traditional question, "Is the soul immortal?" but rather, "in what form?"

Imbert develops a line of thinking that is very original. His notion of the immortality of the soul reflects what can be called a middle way between the Catholic position and what I will refer to as a Neo-Platonic rendition of the afterlife. For Imbert, the self-determination and autonomy that animates human beings can go on to live in a disembodied, pure-soul state. What Imbert's story seems to suggest, however, is that the body only serves as the outward vehicle that allows for a union or interaction with others. The pure soul, on the other hand, acts as the vitality or what amounts to the autonomy that a subject recognizes in itself. Hence the ontological reality that the protagonist encounters after his death is nothing less than surprising. This ontological confusion begins when the protagonist becomes disoriented to find himself "dead." But after the initial shock of death and simultaneously finding himself disembodied in an afterlife, the protagonist's efforts are all geared towards communication with the living. However, after the possibility for communication is exhausted he then begins a campaign of trying to communicate with the dead. But once this too fails, he has no choice but to concentrate on what or who he is now that he is disembodied.

The questions that this story suggests in terms of subjectivity and human autonomy are not only philosophically daring, but also illuminating. Imbert seems to suggest that the spirit or geist that animates human life is often neglected through the material process of human life. He paints a picture whereby the true nature of subjectivity cannot help but to confront itself once that the many distractions of the flesh have been assuaged.

The protagonist in this work, who incidentally remains nameless throughout the story, realizes that he has died only after seeing his own body fall over a chair and unto the floor. After his limp body, which he now stares at, and the chair that he tries holding onto, have both fallen to the floor in the middle of the room, he mutters, "so, this is death?"[1] Thus, the story begins with a philosophical anti-climax, as it were. In this respect the story resembles the closed-room detective genre, this, by inviting the reader to cite the appropriate questions to an answer that is ready at hand. Imbert attacks the question of life after death in a paradoxical but vital manner. Because the story is a work of fiction and not a philosophical treatise, Imbert can sustain the use of the imagination as a further rational tool in metaphysical questioning. It might seem obvious to the discerning reader that from the perspective of life, death, then, is a non-event given that one cannot be conscious of having lost consciousness. The reason for this is that logically the same consciousness that is in the process of being annihilated cannot at the same time remain aware of its own destruction. This state of awareness is precisely what death negates. The protagonist can only realize that he is dead from the perspective of a possible afterlife, but not while in the process of dying, regardless of how little time elapses. The inherent mystery of this momentary transition, Imbert seems to imply, is where all of our hopes and aspirations lie. Let us refer to this view of the afterlife, then, as the common sense view of immortality. This traditional and common sense view perspective is seemingly what most humans hope for. But Imbert quickly juxtaposes our sense of reality.

Enrique Anderson Imbert was born in Argentina in 1910. His literary exploits include novels, essays, and short stories. A substantial number of his literary works utilize paradoxical, if not altogether metaphysical, themes and motifs. Amongst his early novels we can mention *Vigilia* (1934) and *Fuga* (1953). *El Fantasma* originally appeared in *El grimorio*. Bur Imbert is also very well known as a literary critic and historian. He is the author of a very insightful history of Spanish-American literature tilted *Historia de la Literatura Hispanoamericana*, which has appeared in two volumes.

I will suggest that the rendition of the afterlife that Enrique Anderson Imbert proposes is a genuine example of a solipsistic existence, as best as this radical loneliness can be conceived. The story leaves us with several options when trying to pinpoint its

---

1. Gloria Duran & Manuel Duran. *El Mundo Del Mas Allá.* New York: Harcourt Brace Jovanovich, Inc., p. 53.

possible metaphysical implications. Furthermore, because this work is a short story and not a longer fictional work it is not ruled by the novelistic constrains of having to develop the inner workings of many characters. It is, instead, a work that solicits thought and reflection. The reason for my contention has to do with the theme, mood, motif, and the inherent internal conflicts that make up this tale. These are all by their very nature concerns of the thinker par excellence. Another promising aspect of this story as a philosophical case-study of immortality is that in the presence of several "real," that is, differentiated characters, their concerns, hopes and aspirations become a unique and perhaps the appropriate manner to offer an existential treatment of the subject of immortality. In contradistinction to my present proposal, the often-employed analytic manner of dealing with abstract "agents" when we really mean people, and "entities" to mean human beings is not a vital approach to this question. My contention is that such a method goes awry in terms of a humanistic approach to subjectivity, especially where literature is concerned. This analytic method does not take into strict consideration the holistic nature and inner dynamics of the human person. The limitations of this said method are impractical and daunting. It seems that traditional approaches to the question of immortality have been formulated either from a strictly religious viewpoint, or from an overly intellectualized wordplay. Imbert's story, on the other hand, is a fine example of how literature can make its greatest contribution to humanism. *El Fantasma* accomplishes this by posing metaphysical and ontological conditions that are not readily grasped by analytical thinking.

Thus, let the following brief introduction into some of the philosophical implications of literature serve as an introduction to some of the main philosophical themes found in *El Fantasma*. Furthermore, whatever the necessary psychological intentions of the writer, as a creator of stories and in whatever genre that this activity is manifested is not my task to criticize. However, it is the desire if not the responsibility of the speculative thinker to comment on the philosophical implications of a given work when this task is duly warranted. It is my deepest conviction that the role of literature not only remains paramount in terms of an exploration of meaning in human existence, beginning perhaps with wisdom literature, but that this role will increase in the future. The natural marriage of literature and existential philosophy, for instance, will continue to serve as an essential source of philosophical understanding. Part of the reason for this is that the high esteem that has traditionally been attributed to ancient sources in matters of wisdom, meaning, and *Eudaimonia* has eroded as sources of inspiration for contemporary man. Reasons for this displacement are several. But suffice it to say that where often discerning thinkers and writers have now become cynical and nihilistic regarding meaning, the door has been left open for gurus of all kinds and "denominations" to enlighten the public with empty sophisms that are deemed "self help." The role of literature in the future must be that of offering a unitary, humanistic, and well-articulated conception of the human condition. This is a task that, given all current indicators, unfortunately will continue to evade the overly specialized thinker.

This chapter has been organized in the following fashion. In Part I, I offer an account of the problematic that the plot and genre of *El Fantasma* engender. To this I offer a philosophical perspective, but always keeping in place the literary conventions and their importance to the overall cohesion of this literary work. Part II is a short history of some of the major philosophical and religious solutions that have been offered to the question of the immortality of the soul. This is not an exhaustive list by any means, but it does serve as the locus for the metaphysical framework that is relevant to the logical orientation of this essay in lieu of *El Fantasma*. This latter section is crucial to an understanding of Imbert's notion of the immortality of the soul. This brief history of some of the classic renditions of immortality will also allow us to properly situate Imbert's work in the broader spectrum of the philosophical tradition regarding immortality and solipsism. In Part III I develop the argument that Imbert's "El Fantasma" places the human soul in such a surreal and solitary position that can only be interpreted as solipsistic. However, this chapter is not meant as a treatise on solipsism. In this section I also cite some other relevant literary examples of the main themes exhibited in *El Fantasma.*

PART I

Death of the Main Character in El Fantasma

The aforementioned common sense view or what Voltaire has called *le bon sens* is not necessarily that of logic or mathematics, but rather a well-rooted sense of reality that allows man to live constructively. However, Imbert quickly thwarts the orthodox expectations of the laziest readers. Where an afterlife is sought, Imbert instead gives us a closed–in, claustrophobic, and solipsistic nightmare. Instead of a possible communication between the living and the dead we are offered an agonizing language of silence. Also where the common sense view of death garners the hope of a union with the souls of the dead, this possibility, too, quickly evaporates into illusion. Imbert states:

> What a disappointment. I wanted to know how one got to the other world, and I find out that there is no other world.[1]

Having come to terms with this vacuous and painful realization the protagonist then opts to remain in the room where he has died. He looks around in utter amazement to find out that death has not changed a single aspect of what used to be his life. He stares at his own cadaver as if looking in a mirror, only to find himself aged.[2] Once that the initial mystery — the excitement, I dare say, is quenched he wants to return to his former life. Let us keep in mind that as awkward as this last statement may sound he

1. Ibid., p. 53.
2. Ibid., p. 53.

does not anticipate his death in any form. By this I simply mean that
he is not ill. The protagonist is instead surprised by death. The
shock of finding himself dead is a pivotal point in the story; he
doesn't find the kind of afterlife that most people seek. This makes
the magnitude of the shock twofold. It is at this point in the story
that he states:

> Now that I know that there are no angels or abyss on the other
> side, I want to return to my humble abode.[1]

However, it is never explicitly stated what it is that he hoped
to find on the other side. Would it not be sufficient to just simply
arrive there? At this point the protagonist is disappointed by what
he finds. It is after this initial shock that his disembodied soul
attempts to re-enter the body. The narrator states:

> With good humor he went over to his cadaver — empty cage
> — and attempted to enter it again to animate it again.[2]

But this attempt is foiled when in the process his wife enters
the room. "Don't come in," he cries — but without a voice — as she
throws herself, in tears, over his limp body."[3] Apparently unaffected
by her pain, he exclaims, "Be quiet! You have ruined everything," but,
once again, having no voice, his comments to her have become
nothing more than an internal soliloquy.

At this point he wishes that he had closed the door to the room
in order to return to his body without any interruption. Not
convinced that he can pull this off, he begins to think of it as an
"experiment." Realizing that he is trapped in a disembodied state, he
leaves the room, in a sad mood. He has nowhere to go. At this point
he arrives at the startling realization that there is no supernatural
world and therefore no mystery. He then begins to fly around the
room, but discovers that he cannot go through the walls. He leaves
the room through the keyhole, not having any corporal sensation
whatsoever.

---

1. Ibid., p. 53.
2. Ibid., p. 53.
3. Ibid., p. 53.

Next he attends his own funeral alongside his friends and relatives. He even sees the clods of earth descend onto his coffin. All his life he had been a domestic man, always returning home to his wife and daughters after work. Finding no reason to change, he decides to remain in his home to watch over his family.[1] The realization that he cannot flee into the heavens acts as a demarcation point in the story. This is essentially the point that I will refer to as constituting the second part of the story.

During the winter his wife falls ill and he catches himself selfishly hoping that she will soon die, in order that he can be reunited with her. He hopes that they will soon be reunited as souls. His wife does indeed die — but her soul is as invisible to him as he is to his daughters. Now, he is even lonelier, given that he cannot see her. His only comfort is in looking over their daughters. But one day he is horrified to imagine that his house, possibly the entire physical world, might be full of souls. As the years go by his mother-in-law takes care of the orphans. Eventually, he witnesses the death of his three daughters, one by one, unmarried and childless. This is an important part of the plot because it means that the protagonist will no longer have any further ties with the physical world. "The fire of the flesh began to die unlike in other more extended families where it multiplies like a wild fire,"[2] he states. He now begins to imagine his entire family hovering around his house. When his mother-in-law dies, he goes to her coffin and cries, alone. At this point there simply is no one left to unite the family in love. Leaving the house once and for all, he bids his wife and daughters farewell and then goes into the yard and flies off into the night.

The title of this story suggests a ghost. But a ghost in its broader connotation is often that shadowy specter which appears to the living. Moreover, the ghost is a soul of a dead person whom appears to someone. But in this story the spirit or "Fantasma" makes no surprise or ghastly appearance. The connotation of the Spanish

---

1. Ibid., p. 55.
2. Ibid., p. 55.

word *fantasma* has to do with an entity that is equally unknown to others as it is to itself. This, then, is a strong indication that the story is not about a ghost as this manifests itself to the living vis-à-vis the mechanisms employed in the standard ghost story. This is not a ghost story. Imbert does not employ the traditional trappings of the ghost story. In *El Fantasma* there are no haunted places, apparitions, or malicious souls running about molesting the tranquility of mortals as is commonly found in the work of Edgar Allen Poe, Henry James, Wilkie Collins or Sheridan Le Fanu, for instance.

The main point of departure for Imbert instead is the shock that a particular man undergoes to find himself not only dead, but also unenlightened by the apparent lack of any otherworldly wisdom. What seems to be at issue here for Imbert is the plight of man as we make the transition from life into an afterlife, which is not the orthodox or stereotypical one that some people assume is the epitome of our destiny. The emphasis of the story is an exploration of a "what if?" scenario regarding the soul. It is for this reason that the writer employs an omniscient narrator. In this manner the reader is made to see his own possible future through empathy for the protagonist. Thus the pathos that Imbert makes us feel is our own. The realization that to live forever as a disembodied soul without the possibility of communication with either the living or the dead is Imbert's very rendition of hell. However, if one grants that this oppressive solitude serves merely as an allegorical rendition of hell, then, a further disclaimer is necessary. Hell in this story is an agonizing state of being much like the portrait of hell that Sartre paints in *No Exit*. Where in *No Exit* the characters suffer both emotionally and psychologically, the main character in Imbert's work has no sensations, thus his suffering is purely existential. Imbert's rendition of hell is hell as loneliness. While I understand that it is not the writer's responsibility to work out the possible philosophical implications in a work of fiction, we must make clear for our purpose here that in this case the protagonist cannot suffer sensually, given that he has no body. But what else is left, then?

Since the story does not end with his physical death, we are left with the reality that this particular individual continues to exist as a soul. Sartre's play makes use of both external as well as internal conflict because the work is about people, as they exist as mortals whom must deal with the existence of others. Conversely, Imbert can only showcase internal conflict in what is perhaps its ultimate meaning, incommunicable loneliness. Imbert builds loneliness as his main motif, one that creates an asphyxiating solipsistic mood. But we shall further develop this notion of solipsism in Part III. Now let us turn our attention to a brief understanding of the traditional significance of the soul in the major religions and in western philosophy. This can enlighten us as to the role that the soul plays in this story.

PART II

A Brief History of the Soul and Immortality

Most primitive societies seem to have a belief in a soul that animates the body while a person was alive, but which leaves the body at the time of death. In this respect the soul is seen as a life-substance or anima. However, in given primitive societies the soul is additionally believed to be autonomous, that is, a separate entity that can exist on its own outside the body. In terms of documented civilizations some of the very best examples of this are found in the Egyptians and the Sumerians. Gilgamesh meets with Utnapishtin, who has discovered immortality, in order to gain understanding from the old man's secret.

Interestingly, the soul in some early civilizations is also said to leave the body during sleep, possibly during the dreaming stage, returning to the body afterwards. These primitive conceptions of the soul are seen as animating factors in the life of an animal or person. James Frazer, writer of the *Golden Bough*, refers to primitive notions of the soul as: "the animal inside the animal, the man inside the man, is the soul."[1] Moreover, the body, regardless of the deformation that it must endure, does not affect this soul. In this respect it seems clear that the soul has more often than not been seen as a separate entity from the body. One aspect of animism, for instance, is a belief that disembodied spirits make their way into the bodies of sleeping people whose souls have left during the dream state. Such a belief is documented in the work of the nineteenth-century anthropologist E.B. Tylor. There was also a belief that the soul returns to the site of the dead body, and this was perhaps the beginning of the tradition of bringing food to the dead that is prevalent in many cultures even to the present. The food is an offering to protect the dead from the unknown. Some cultures have even suggested that the soul enters another body, which is a reflection of the moral quality of the life left behind. In other words, a better body for good souls, while bad bodies are reserved for bad souls.

The three main revealed religions of the ancient world, Zoroastrianism, Judaism and Christianity, all have a sophisticated notion of the soul. In Zoroastrianism, the prophet Zoroaster, who was born in Azerbaijan (at that time part of Persia) in the seventh to sixth centuries BCE, is one of the first to mention the notion of a final punishment. It is believed that at around the age of thirty, the prophet had a vision of the archangel of good intention, Vohu Mana, who directed the young man to the presence of the wise lord Ahura Mazda, where he was taught the principles of goodness. Human life in Zoroastrianism is equated with a moral value that will come to be weighed in the afterlife, thus bringing about the belief that "the deceitful person misses the true conception of the honest man. His soul shall vex him at the bridge of the judge."[2]

In Judaism and Christianity, the soul is viewed as the life-giving source of the differentiated individual-body. This soul is said

---

1. Frazer. *The Golden Bough*. p. 120.
2. S.A. Nigosian. *The Zoroastrian Faith: Tradition & Modern Research*. Montreal: McGill-Queen's University Press, 1993, p. 23.

to eventually return to its immaterial form where it is judged for its incarnate actions. Of course, the body in these religions is viewed as sacred as well.

For the early Greeks, the notion of the soul was chiefly manifested in Pantheism, or the belief that all nature is alive. Philosophically speaking, the pre-Socratics were the very first thinkers to give this belief a rather systematic and rational treatment. According to Anaximenes, the soul is made of rarefied air (ether). This ether is said to keep the universe together. Pythagoras, the great mathematician and mystic, offers the belief in a soul as a moral or ethical component by attributing the degree of happiness in the afterlife more or less in proportion to the life once lived. This belief also regulates the temporal life of man thus suggesting that order, form, and logos should rule human life. For Heraclitus, the soul is seen as a kind of fire that is ever changing, but that is never destroyed. In Empedocles' estimation, the human soul enters another body after death and continues to live. This is known as the transmigration of souls. This belief is also the basis of what the Orphic religion proclaimed. The doctrine of Atomism, which mainly consisted of the work of Leucippus, the founder of Atomism (and subsequently of his follower Democritus, according to both Aristotle and Theophrastus), offers a materialistic rendition of the soul. In Atomism the soul, like every other aspect of the *kosmos*, is composed of atoms that are indestructible. For the atomist, the soul disintegrates at the time of death and, being thus scattered, leaves no identifiable characteristics.

Both Socrates and his pupil Plato view the soul as pre-existing prior to its inception into a body. Their notion of the soul is one that is best expressed in terms of anamnesis or what the ancient Greeks referred to as remembering. In this respect the task of the soul is to remember or come to terms with the understanding that it already possesses all the learning necessary in this life. Plato argues that prior to its manifestation in the flesh, the soul was in the presence of the ultimate or perfect form, the Good. In fact, Plato equates the body with a kind of prison where the soul, which has witnessed the archetypal forms of all things prior to birth, begins to lose its way in the material realm.

Aristotle attributes the existence of the soul to reason or intelligence, which conceptualizes the meaning of existence. Aristotle views the portion of the soul that he attributes to creative reason as being an immaterial substance that survives the death of the body. Furthermore, the soul in Aristotle can be said to resemble a portion of the unmoved mover as pure mind. Later developments concerning the notion of the human soul can be observed to become offshoots of these basic tenets. For instance, during the subsequent neo-Platonism thinkers such as Origen, Plotinus, and the entire Patristic period and leading up to Boethius, the body-soul dualism becomes a standard philosophical belief. For St. Augustine the soul does not exist prior to its material existence. Saint Thomas Aquinas views the soul as forming a spiritual body that continues to live eternally.

After Descartes the dichotomy of object-subject mind (soul)-body with few exceptions became a staple element in the work of philosophers up until the development of Positivism by Auguste Comte in the early years of the nineteenth century. After Comte, all other forms of materialism have either dismissed the idea of the soul altogether or have re-constituted it as a chimerical function of the brain or something pertaining to an epiphenomenon. As an interesting footnote to all fundamental beliefs in the immortality of the soul, after the advent of the stringent materialism of the late nineteenth century there begins a resurgence of belief in the immortality of the soul in the form of spiritualism. Spiritualism saw its mainstay in the work of Madame Blavatsky, especially in the excitement that her founding of the Theosophical Society generated. Conan Doyle spent the last ten years of his life writing and lecturing on spiritualism, and Mark Twain became captivated by the subject towards the end of his life. In philosophical circles, the prominent American thinker William James and the Frenchman, Gabriel Marcel were also very much involved with the question of human immortality.

PART III

Solipsism = (Latin Solus, alone, ipse, self).

It is a safe bet that proponents of solipsism in philosophical circles are very few. One of the main reasons for this is that such a doctrine appears to be counterintuitive. To proclaim oneself alone is perhaps best served by an understanding that to do so is to accept the following two points: 1) That others, that is, beings much like ourselves, once occupied our immediate vicinity (by which I mean our consciousness) and no longer do so; or, 2) That one has rejected the existence of the other wholeheartedly, on epistemological grounds. In any case the irrefutable common sense assumption to most people outside some philosophical circles is that other sentient beings exist besides us. But it is not so much this reality that the solipsist denies, even though he must contend with this point, but rather the notion that we can attain any degree of certainty at all. To the solipsist the presence of the other can only be known in its apparent and choking absence or what amounts to a negation.

But even then, how can Imbert's protagonist be said to be in a solipsistic state of being? If we take the aforementioned definition of solipsism as a strictly logical proposition then clearly the answer is that he cannot be. The problem is exacerbated by the condition that as a doctrine metaphysical solipsism asserts that there are: 1) No other beings or subjective "I's" beside oneself, and 2) That there is no external world. Besides this view there is also an epistemological form of solipsism, which in a sense serves as a "softer" version of the more absolute metaphysical type. Epistemological solipsism does not necessarily assert that only "I" exist, but that the only true knowledge that one can ever have is knowledge of the content of one's own consciousness. As a point of contention solipsism must remain logically nonsensical or incommunicable. By definition the claim is that at worse there are no others with whom one can communicate and at best that two minds cannot interact. Descartes is the first thinker to question whether there is an external world or if, as he writes concerning the existence of others "are they inventions of my mind?"[1] To this general assertion Kant rebuttals that solipsism is "a scandal to philosophy."[2] But is that strict and rigorous logical proposition the only manner through which we can appropriate solipsism? A subsequent treatment of these Cartesian doubts can be seen in the work of Bishop Berkeley and other idealists.

In Imbert's story, however, the plot does not showcase the main character claiming or believing that he is the only existent reality. On the contrary, he finds himself alone precisely because he is separated from his family. His state of loneliness is contrasted with a previous state of conviviality with others. Imbert seems to emphasize that the real complication begins when the protagonist does become truly alone and unable to communicate with the dead, the living or any higher being, e.g. God. Even though this story appears to be deceptively simple, the philosophical complexities that it entertains quickly become evident. But length alone does not give one an accurate indication of the level of sophistication of a written work; certainly not this one.

The protagonist comes to the fearful realization that he is in fact totally alone. This coerced reflection forces him to come to terms with the immediate grasp of his conscious "I." As an important point of contention we must ask whether, once that the protagonist has lost his body, he also loses his senses? Moreover, if he is said not to possess any of the five senses, what other faculties remain to allow him the possibility of knowledge? Possessing no physical body, sensation ceases. This being the case, we can only attribute the understanding that the protagonist still possesses

---

1. *Encyclopedia of Philosophy*. Edited by Paul Edwards. p. 488.
2. Ibid., p. 489.

regarding this state of disembodiment as a mere noeton or that which is capable of being grasped solely through the intellect. This, then, in a few words is exactly the kind of metaphysical questioning which most arguments for the existence of the soul contend with. The state of the soul as we find it in Imbert's work is that of pure form. As pure form, the soul (psyche) can have knowledge of the sensual world. For instance, in Parmenides and Plato we find that trust in the senses is not only misleading at best, but also detrimental to true knowledge. The body according to these two thinkers is a sort of prison where the soul is trapped, and the goal is to understand human reality conceptually.

These alleged complications in the ability of the disembodied soul to communicate with the living are already noted in ancient culture. Even in pre-philosophical literature and ritual the problem of the noeton and the senses cannot be ignored. The missionary J. Warneck who was able to closely study the spiritualist religion of the Batak people of the Malay Archipelago writes in regard to the manner in which the spirit of the dead or the *begu* communicates with the living: "The begu of the dead person cannot converse directly with the living because he has no body. This is why he must borrow the body of a living person when he desires to converse with his descendants."[1]

While it remains true that such accounts contain a great deal of suggestibility, they nevertheless help to illustrate the problem of the loss of the senses in Imbert's story.

Let us take a look at another literary example that closely resembles *El Fantasma*. In Emile Zola's short story *The Death of Olivier Becaille*, the main character dies, becomes a spectator at his own funeral and is eventually too cognizant of his own burial as he suffers through a living entombment. About this hellish circumstance he utters, "Eternity is not of longer duration than one second spent in nihility."[2] When he manages to return from his

---

1. T.K. Oesterreich. *Possession: Demoniacal & Other Among Primitive Races, In Antiquity, The Middle Ages, and Modern Times.* Secaucus: The Citadel Press, 1966 p. 268.

"death," he is saddened to see that his wife is about to remarry. He walks the streets pensively pondering whether to return home, but finally opts against this. His reasoning is that he does not wish to disturb the happiness that his widow has found. At this point he no longer fears death but rather only loneliness. He states, "Death no longer frightens me, but it does not seem to care for me now that I have no motive in living; and I have been forgotten upon earth."[1] A more recent example of this same theme is found in Javier Marias' short story collection, *When I was Mortal*.

The notion of solipsism that I am proposing only applies to the state of being of the protagonist once he has died. Even though his prior existence was one where he was surrounded by people, it is his disembodied solitary existence that concerns us. My point is simply that his being, that is, his former essence as a mortal being no longer applies to his current condition as a disembodied soul. The existence of his being as pure soul has changed. In a similar vein, Schopenhauer compares the act of death as a return to the nothingness, the eternity from which we have come. He writes in *The Vanity of Existence*: "That which has been exists no more; it exists as little as that which has never been. But of everything that exists you may say, in the next moment, that it has been. Hence something of great importance in our past is inferior to something of little importance in our present, in that the latter is a reality, and related to the former as something to nothing."[2]

This Schopenhauerian perspective is analogous to my argument in so far as it drastically differentiates between two radical and substantial changes in being. But perhaps this is where this voluntary comparison ends. The protagonist in *El Fantasma* cannot forget his corporal existence. For this reason his historicity

---

2. Emile Zola. "The Death of Oliver Becaille." *The Works of Emile Zola.* Roslyn, New York: Black's Readers Service Company, 1928. p. 58.

1. Ibid., p. 65.

2. Arthur Schopenhauer. "The Vanity of Existence." *The Works of Arthur Schopenhauer: The Wisdom of Life and Other Essays.* Roslyn, New York: Black's Readers Service Company, 1928. p. 229.

cannot be overlooked. This is why he is forced to compare the two states that he has now experienced. In light of this possibility, let us now attempt to decipher several of the inherent metaphysical possibilities found in the story itself.

First, we must consider the practical meaning of love, a force that unites and gives meaning to all human endeavors. Imbert clearly states that the main character is a very domestic man. By this he seems to be setting up the conditions whereby the reader understands that this man's total world revolves around his three daughters and his wife. There is no mention of friends or acquaintances, only his family. In other words, his family is his world. Is this love diminished somehow if a reunification is brought about in the afterlife? Imbert's literary scope and depth of perspective is in keeping with what amounts to a realistic understanding of the "actual" life of his characters. The author's concern for the practical questions of human life is seen through his vision of one man's life and death. Suffice it to say for our purpose in this essay that love plays an important role in the overall conception of the human life that Imbert has supplied us with. Perhaps it can be argued that the very same conditions that exist for the loved one in death can also hold true in life. Furthermore, it can be argued that *El Fantasma* is simply a tale of loneliness. However, such a rendition would merely make use of the element of the protagonist's death as a metaphorical condition to illustrate his state of loneliness. This, however, would eliminate all importance to the questioning concerning the afterlife. If the aforementioned possibility is granted the overriding meaning imparted in this story would then be that human life is not worth living in isolation from others especially where love may reside.

My second point is that if we allow the afterlife to remain the main point of emphasis in the story then our concentration must remain with the existence of the disembodied soul and not with his prior mortal life. Again, it can be argued that because Imbert, much like Borges, has written a large number of these metaphysical stories, we can indeed seriously consider the question of the immortality of the soul as being a predominant theme in his work. We can even suggest that the protagonist suffers in a state of "limbo" where he awaits the moral questioning that he must satisfy in order to enter the heavenly realm. Or perhaps his internal torment, which is manifested in his loneliness is no other than the result of a dubious moral predicament, one which cannot be erased until a catharsis has taken place. As George Santayana writes in one of his sonnets, the meaning of heaven is simply to be at peace with oneself and with things.

This state of confusion, which in spiritualist circles is often referred to as limbo, would explain the sense of loss that Imbert's protagonist feels. This state of being, this being suspended between a world that is neither otherworldly nor Earthly has made many entries into world literature including in Dante's *Inferno* and William Butler Yeats' *Purgatory*. In the latter work the characters involved are simply a young boy, an old man and an abandoned house. Yet in many respects the characters in Yeats' work are man's historicity and a heavy, guilty conscious. At the beginning of *El Fantasma* the protagonist possesses none of these burdensome characteristics. The main character does not realize that he has died and refuses to go on his way. Instead, he remains in his home as a sentinel watching over his family. Perhaps his refusal to depart the corporal world only adds to his loneliness. This is a significant point because at the very end of the story, after the death of his last loved one, he does leave into the void of space.

The gulf that inhibits communication between the living and the dead and the dead with each other also brings to mind Miguel de Unamuno's 1914 novel *Niebla* (Mist). In *Mist* man is existentially cut off from his peers by an incessant nihility, thus the mist which engulfs man along with all his hopes. Unamuno argues that the best antidote to the "tragic sense of life" that takes control of all our aspirations is found in the hope of an eternal life. The final word on human life, however, Unamuno unabashedly tells us is that the consciousness that establishes the I-pole of human existence proves nothing other than that human existence, which is essentially always grasped as a unique subjectivity is no less than a mystery. Imbert's story, too, leaves the reader with this same sense of philosophical mystery.

Another interesting point to ponder is whether Imbert is suggesting that all subjective, thus existential, experiences are always essentially a private matter. But if such is the case, how then does one communicate both our joy and pain? According to the solipsistic position communication is impossible. In the story the protagonist does not talk. This is why there is no first person account of the psychological make-up of the character. Furthermore, as a consequence of this the author never has to use the pronouns "I", "they", and "you" as a literary device. This compounds the philosophical problem while getting the author off the hook, as it were. Again, I must reiterate that while the classical arguments against solipsism tend to be analytic in scope; few have taken a "language-free" approach to the problem. What I mean by this is that while most of the wrangling that goes on in this type of argument stresses logical coherence, I, on the contrary, consider this problem like any philosophical problem in terms of what the ancient Greeks called phenomena or the appearance of reality and not solely with concern for language. The word phenomenology was first used by Johan Heinrich Lambert (1728-1777), a contemporary of Kant when he said that the aforementioned would be "the theory of illusion."[1] In separating the notion of appearance (phenomena) from the 'things-in-themselves' (noumena), Kant concludes that the mind can only know appearances or what amounts to the surface structure of reality. Consider what is meant when Hamlet in Act I, Scene V tells Horatio that "there are more things in heaven and Earth Horatio than are dreamt of in your philosophy." Hamlet's implication is clear: that perhaps human existence is composed of equally ineffable essences.

But as I have already alluded, the main issues of solipsism as conceived by most philosophers are often decided in technical

---

1. *Encyclopedia of Philosophy*, p. 135.

wrangling over self-referential language. The analytic thinker presses the paradoxical point that solipsism cannot be true precisely because in order to prove this ontological reality it must first be communicated. This assertion states that if solipsism is to remain intelligible it cannot also simultaneously remain a valid proposition. The logical entailment here is that if we are totally alone then how can we communicate anything at all? However the proponent of solipsism must counter this argument by pointing out that this argument, much like any other must have a logical semantic structure. This logical language is philosophically juxtaposed by Pedro Calderon de la Barca's classic 1635 play, *La Vida es Sueño (Life Is a Dream)* where he writes in reference to the "internal stream of life" that is felt as conscious life: For the world we live in is so curious that to live is but to dream. And all that's happened to me tells me that while he lives man dreams what he is until he wakens.

> I dream that I am here manacled in this cell, and I dreamed I saw myself before, much better off. What is life? A frenzy. What is life? An illusion, fiction, passing shadow, and the greatest good the merest dot, for all of life's a dream, and dreams themselves are only part of dreaming (xxix).[1]

But in *El Fantasma* the author remains consistent in his approach to the protagonist's loneliness. Throughout the work the omniscient narrator makes explicit reference to the protagonist only three times. Once he refers to the protagonist as "he said." The other two times the narrator simply states, "He thought." Yet the greatest obstacle facing solipsism, as a truly valid philosophical deduction is the demand placed on reality by proponents of linguistic analysis. However, the condition of extirpating a given metaphysical proposition because it does not readily meet a pre-established analytical prerequisite is naïve. This staunch, fact-oriented conception of reality can indeed help us in deciphering the more somber attributes of data or as Auguste Comte called it, "facts." Yet

---

1. Pedro Calderón de la Barca. *La Vida Es Sueno*. p. xxix.

there still remains a most serious question as to how much of this concentration on language is truly philosophical discourse at all. And still furthermore, is this hyper-analytic process truly comparable with reality proper? It appears evident that once the possibility of reflection concerning metaphysical matters is wholly eliminated, what remains in many cases is simply an epistemological shell. Epistemology, like the scientific method, is most effective as a competent method of asking questions in terms of "how?" while metaphysical questions are always seeking to uncover the transcendent and more foundational question, "why?" But the logical relationship that gives meaning to inanimate cold facts does not in itself inhere in the facts. It can be argued that the relationship that exists amongst facts is always a logical deduction first and foremost. Karl Jaspers pays close attention to this particular problem by observing that positivist thinkers, including scientists in their many varied fields confuse the world of fact with that of reality. Reality, Jaspers argues, is known through what he calls the "encompassing" (das Umgreifende) or experiencing the total and ultimate nature of being as this is manifested in our life. Science, on the other hand, he tells us is a form of symbols — ciphers, he calls them (chiffren) that even though useful in grounding our existence in practical understanding cannot offer us a complete rendition of human reality. This assertion is particularly telling when we consider that this man who is best known as an existentialist philosopher was also a physician. In terms of epistemology, Jaspers' as well as Imbert's concern is not so much with an objective epistemology, but rather with establishing the primacy of subjectivity.

Having considered some of the inherent problems of solipsism, let us now turn our attention to the reality that the protagonist actually occupies. The protagonist in *El Fantasma* finds himself in a world of solitude. The narrator in this case can only be interpreted as a defused and omniscient God. Only God as a sub specie aeternitas can understand the perspective of the protagonist. However, while God may be conscious of the protagonist as a soul, the protagonist cannot communicate with god. This is a viable avenue for the author to take given that the reader shares the understanding of the narrator. The reader in contradistinction to the protagonist does not find himself in a state of solipsism. But the tantalizing question "what if?" becomes intractable. The nature of such a possibility is the driving force behind this story. The importance of the narrator in this case is that in offering a view of the internal conflicts that inhere in the protagonist we are also offered a view of ourselves. This is a common occurrence in literature, except that in most literary works the claim is not made that the protagonist is radically alone, but rather only existentially alone. This is clearly the case with Defoe's *Robinson Crusoe*, for instance, where the sole concentration of the author throughout most of that novel is with an exploration of the existential, moral and emotional make-up of the protagonist. While it is true that *Robinson Crusoe* is a spatial-temporal being and the protagonist in Imbert's work is not, the qualitative existential condition of each man remain the same. However, the import and severity of Imbert's particular problem in narrating this story is more than descriptive, but rather also diagnostic in scope. The reason for this is that the protagonist cannot compare the here-and-now with the afterlife, if we are to grant the solipsistic position a credible status. The protagonist is alone and locked-up in a reality that knows no other possibilities. Also we should clarify that the word "solipsism" itself in this particular context becomes problematic as well as paradoxical. The word is descriptive of a radical and trenchant state of being. Yet this word, like any other word is meant for public consumption. Except that in Imbert's case we must notice that because of the primal state of being in question the word solipsism, even though not tropic in intent does however have limitations. This, I believe is where most of the confusion lies with this metaphysical line of reasoning. If one argues, as Derrida for instance that philosophical language or what he refers to as "white mythology" is no more than metaphorical in scope then the essence of the question simply becomes a blurred obscurantist language game. But if we assert, like Paul Ricoeur, that language is the dialectical culmination of intentionality then we allow language to act as a crucial aspect of a greater gestalt. It is possible for a thinker to separate the use of language as a tool of communication amongst sentient beings from the ineffable impenetrability that an ultimate reality such as this entails. In discussing the nature of existential questions vis-à-vis the epistemological limits of the scientific method, Etienne Gilson writes, in *God and Philosophy*: "the marked antipathy of modern science toward the notion of efficient cause is intimately related to the nonexistential character of scientific explanations. It is of the essence of an efficient cause that it makes something be, or exist. Since the relation of effect to cause is an existential and a nonanalytical one, it appears to the scientific mind as a sort of scandal, which must be eliminated."[1]

A final point of consideration about *El Fantasma* is the suggestion that love, as an existential and subjectively qualitative essence, gives human life a true and sustaining meaning. After the protagonist's family members have all died he then leaves the confines of his house and retires into the darkness of space. A central configuration of this story is that Imbert does not make use of any singular mention of Christian theology or symbolism. There is never any explicit mention of God. He does not place his protagonist in an afterlife where he enjoys the presence of other departed souls. The story does not have a single reference to heaven or hell. Also, he does not remain in his home to watch over his family given that he is impotent to undertake such a task and they cannot take notice of him anyhow. To them, he is effectively dead. He simply chooses to remain in his former home because to "be" with them as a spectator of their being is a much higher value than to be totally alone. The parallels of his staying in his home are consistent with the belief that love is a motivating factor in living. This notion of love is analogous to the love that is forged between mortals.

---

1. Etienne Gilson. *God and Philosophy*. New Haven: Yale University Press, 1941. p. 19.

Thus, in concluding, I must point out that Imbert apparently stresses the value of a worldly existence in the presence of the loved one more than the possibility of an afterlife. Nevertheless he does present a vision of an asphyxiatingly lonely afterlife for his protagonist, where communication with other souls is impossible. This, however, is a kind of tease where one is asked to truly understand the intricacies of that which we wish for. He seems to be asking: what good is the immortality of the soul if such an existence does not include any further communion with the loved one, either living or dead? Perhaps Imbert has T.S. Eliot's belief in mind that the world ends not in a bang but with a whimper. This whimper is perhaps so delicate that we do not notice it once it has taken place. If this is the case, then, this whimper can be said of both the autonomy of the living as well as the loneliness of the disembodied soul.[1] Fortunately, Imbert is only suggesting a variation of a possible reality.

---

1. For a very fine study of the many different possibilities for the existence of an afterlife see: Arthur S. Berger's *Aristocracy of the Dead: New Findings in Postmortem Survival.* McFarland & Company, Inc., Publishers: Jefferson, North Carolina. Berger's argument is tantamount to saying that the very same differences that pertain to individuals in human life conceivably pertain to the existence of the soul in the afterlife. This work is indispensable to anyone interested in this question.

CHAPTER 6. SUBJECTIVITY AND PHILOSOPHICAL REFLECTION IN JEAN COCTEAU'S ORPHEUS TRILOGY

> Everything burns and consumes itself. Life itself is the result of combustion. Man's contribution is to leave himself a trail of lovely embers, some of which remain glowing; through these embers the past is revealed in the form of presence; it can be seen a little in its true aspect. For these embers (or works) draw on an imperceptible human essence that is not subject to our standards of measurement. Since they will be here tomorrow when we no longer will be, they must overlap with what we call the future, giving us a vague sensation of fixity, of permanence.
> — Jean Cocteau

Jean Cocteau's artistic vision of the poetic vocation and the poet's struggle to make his essence known in the objective world is a reoccurring theme of his films and books. Cocteau invests his treatment of subjectivity with a sincerity and vital sensibility, I will contend, that is arguably much more effective in exploring this subject matter than most strictly academic "philosophical" works which have embraced this problem.[1] The reasons for this view are many. But it remains undeniably the case that the foundational aspect of Cocteau's philosophical reflection is the conviction that man as a differentiated and subjective entity cannot be abstracted.

Fundamental to Cocteau's work is the metaphysical and existential postulate that the essence and purpose of philosophical reflection is to arrive at self-knowledge. Another reason for this view has to do with the phenomenological quality of cinema.

Cinema takes the immediacy that is human experience and places it on display as an object for reflection. In doing so it makes this immediacy a testament to the subject's intuition of the passage of time. Another reason is that because cinema cannot be conceived as being other than a visual form of narrative, the subject-I always confronts itself from what, in a practical vein is an objective distance. But confrontation with this detached, objective space is representative of the time it takes man to reflect on his immediacy. The photographic qualities of cinema allow its participation in human affairs to serve as a perfect existential timekeeper. But because psychological time is a phenomenological lived-experience and not necessarily a reflective one, cinema presents human experience with a unique view of the past as a reflected immediacy. Cocteau's notion of the "imperceptible human essence, which is not subject to quantifiable measurement, is composed of poetic and intuitive sagacity and the will that is required to execute it.[1]

The legend of Orpheus the singer and animal charmer serves as the ground of Cocteau's metaphysics. Orpheus, more or less a contemporary of the Persian prophet Zoroaster, is credited with

---

1. Cocteau is an example of a thinker who refused to have his wings clipped by academic convention. Like Unamuno and Camus, for instance, he makes his life a vital problem for reflection. Whatever his conclusions may turn out to be, he leaves an indelible mark on human concerns. The same can be said of many other writers who follow in this tradition, like: Giovanni Papini, José Gironella, Octavio Paz, José Ortega y Gasset and Czeslaw Milosz. Such thinkers have demonstrated that specialization may be a necessary evil in the hard sciences, but that it is a detrimentally myopic view in the humanities. Gironella argues that Julian Marias' ability to unify philosophy with the past and present, for instance, is a sign that the true thinker is much more than just an intellect, but rather an artisan of ideas. See: José Maria Gironella. *Los fantasmas de mí cerebro.* Barcelona : Editorial Planeta, 1972, p.357.

1. *Diary of an Unknown.* Translated by Jesse Browner. New York: Paragon House, 1991. p. 213. Julian Marias explains this very clearly when he writes in *Philosophy as Dramatic Theory:* "A philosophical doctrine, if it is philosophical, is responding to a human need to orient oneself, to know what to guide oneself by in relation to reality." p. 55.

being the founder of the Orphic religion. Thus the essential point to consider in Cocteau's work is the visionary initiation that, like his religious counterpart, the poet must seek in order to avoid a life of futility. The task of the poet, then, is to search for that inner understanding that, unlike Sisyphus in antiquity releases the poet from the tedium of modernity.

In Cocteau's Orpheus film trilogy, a modern day poet reflects on the existential suffering that poets must undergo in order to earn their right to exert the personal expression that is indicative of genuine subjective autonomy. From this inner struggle Cocteau garners his notion of immortality that is such a central ingredient in the poet's task. Hence subjectivity and immortality cannot be separated in his films precisely because that is the natural order that the poetic vision demands. Cocteau envisions the role of the poet to be a saver of his own existential constitution. Immortality is achieved by an act of will that transforms the subjective essence into a timeless and transcendent objectivity. All Cocteau's films can be construed as meditations on self-understanding.

Cocteau's use of autobiographical, subjective and Orphic themes render aesthetic vision a philosophical respectability that, with several exceptions including the work of Pound, Eliot, Milosz, and Brodsky, to name a few, is all but absent in twentieth century poetics. The fusion of Orpheus the Greek singer with Orpheus the modern day poet is an effective way of grounding aesthetics in metaphysical reflection. Cocteau's use of music, sound, sculpture, literature and poetry allow his work to attain a unified ethos that comes close to Wagner's dream of a complete art form. Versatility of form was no doubt Cocteau's greatest gift. Moreover, I will contend that the use of ancient myth allows Cocteau the freedom to remind post-modern man that the poetic/philosophical vocation is an ethic. The role of all genuinely autonomous subjectivity is to toil with the often inflexibility of the categorical imperative in human affairs. The profound undercurrent and raison d'etre of Cocteau's work is always to uncover the nature of what he considers to be "the plural lie." [1]

I

Blood of a Poet (*Le Sang D'un Poete*, 1930) is Cocteau's first film. The film essentially poses the ancient question: "How much must an artist suffer for his artistic vision?" As such, this film, like all of his work, is an intense philosophical exploration of the nature of human subjectivity. The metaphysical foundation of this film, as is equally true of the other two installments in this trilogy, *Orpheus* (1950) and *Testament of Orpheus* (1959) is a testament to Cocteau's inherent philosophical vocation. Jean Cocteau (1889-1963), who is also very well known and respected as a poet, essayist and novelist infuses his work with a reflective palpability that is second to no other film director of his day and age or today. Cocteau's films showcase a delicate and intricate handling of classical themes and motifs, which some populist's critics have called "highbrow." But this charge is leveled by pedestrian critics who demand that an artist "commit" his vocation and vision solely to commentary on the nature of social/ political reality. Instead, his films can be conceived to be the celluloid counterparts of moving maxims. The viewer gets a clear indication of this concern for the nature of subjectivity right from the opening sequence, when a quote is shown which reads:

> Every poem is a coat of arms, it must be deciphered. So much blood, so many tears, in exchange for these axes...these heraldic reds ... these unicorns ... these torches ... these towers, these mort-lets ... these seed-beds of stars ... these azure fields.[1]

These quotations appear in the opening scenes of the film; they were very commonly used as plot synopsis in films of the silent era. Even though this film is not silent, the quotes instead work as prose poems that Cocteau uses to guide the direction and thematic of the film. For example, the reference made to "these towers" is a central allusion of the film. At the start of the film a very tall and solitary

---

1. *Diary of an Unknown.* p.10.
1. *Blood of a Poet.* 1930. (Film).

industrial chimney is seen toppling down. But this scene is immediately interrupted by the film's narrative and is not resumed until the end of the film. Perhaps the true importance of the collapsing tower is that it signifies the eventual fall of the solitary artist, both in terms of individual mortality and in the overall understanding of the critics.

Cocteau's work always strives for a detailed analysis of the inner world of the artist as an individual who possesses a prescriptive and singular vision of reality. His major concern is always one that is painstakingly fraught over with the question of the role of individuality in society. This very question is evoked in diverse manners throughout his work. Cocteau nonetheless always offers a definite answer to this question by concentrating on the life and inner world of the artist. He addresses this concern by asserting that in the life of the individual, subjectivity remains the highest reality attainable by man. He infuses his signature classical erudition into this very modern question. That he should attempt to answer this question through an exploration of classical themes and motifs — in short — through mythological humanism seems an appropriate avenue. Through the use of Greek and Roman mythology he can explore themes that post-modernity has effectively given up on.

In 1953, ten years prior to his death, Cocteau wrote *Journal d'un inconnu*, a book of the most French of genres: the essay. Despite the fact that at this time Cocteau was already well known as a novelist, playwright and film director he called this work *Diary of an Unknown*. This title serves as a clear indication of the concerns that he envisioned as encircling, yet ennobling the inner constitution of the artist. In an essay from this book titled *Invisibility*, he writes of the poet.

> Naturally, he consoles himself with the illusion that his work is grounded in some more concrete mystery. But this hope comes from the fact that every man is a night (harbors a night) that an artist's task is to bring that night into the light of day, and that this secular night provides a comforting extension of man's severe

135

limitations. Man thereby becomes a sort of sleeping cripple, dreaming that he can walk.[1]

The opening scene in *Blood of a Poet* presents a young man painting, while in the background the canons of Fontenoy are heard. As this is taking place a modern painting of a woman begins to move her eyes and lips. A few scenes later this same mouth appears on his hands as he washes them in a basin. The caption reads: "Everything from a picture where the naked hand had contracted it like leprosy, the drowned mouth seemed to expire in a small zone of white light."[2]

After this incident the mouth begins to move its lips, only now it does so in silence. When it finally does manage to speak, it simply utters: "Air." The mouth wants air after the painter had drowned it in the basin. Next, he puts the displaced mouth on his own, as the first episode of the film comes to an end. The immediate suggestion to be gathered from this encounter is that the muse of art and inspiration cannot be silenced.

Blood of a Poet takes as its starting point the notion that the immortality that the artist attains can only come as the result of his self-sacrificing will, which transcends his Earthly role. The importance of this conviction in Cocteau's work clearly takes the will of the artist and his public persona to be unequally proportioned. An early indication of this is witnessed in a caption that reads: "The author dedicates this ribbon of allegories to the memory of Pisanello, of Paolo Uccello, of Andrea del Castagno, painters of blazonry and of enigmas."[3]

The second episode begins by asking the question: "Do walls have ears?" Here the significance of mirrors, which will become such a Cocteau film staple later in *Orpheus*, appears for the first time.

Entering another dimension through the mirror, the artist begins to float through an abyss of darkness. The contrast between

---

1. *Diary of an Unknown.* p. 9.
2. *Blood of a Poet.*
3. Ibid.

light and dark resembles a celluloid image of a chiaroscuro painting. Within this abyss he encounters the "Hotel de Folies Dramatiques." This hotel of human and historical folly is just one of Cocteau's many satiric ways of snubbing the many examples of the stupidity that is so prevalent in human history. Here, a comparison with Erasmus' *Praise of Folly* and Voltaire's *Candid* quickly come to mind. One of these human follies is narcissism. Peeping through a keyhole, he sees a Mexican man being shot by a firing squad. The film is then reversed and the man is shot once again. Moving along the corridor in this gallery of follies, he looks through another door where he encounters "the mysteries of China"; someone is smoking a pipe. Another door reveals a little girl and a woman inside the room as the little girl floats up to the ceiling, in a finely tuned representation of his use of modern technology. By the time that he reaches the fourth door the room becomes a repository of surreal images. The satiric implications of these scenes can be read as: "Try making sense of the world, if you can."

At the end of the film there appears a pronouncement that reads: "The path is long," thus citing and emphasizing Cocteau's notion of the "mortal tedium of immortality." A scene of the chimney-tower finally falling to the ground follows these two short quotes. *Blood of a Poet* is a film that critiques ordinary experience vis-à-vis the subjective world of the artist. But Cocteau's main point ought not to be lost on the struggle of the artist to rise above critics and the general public. Instead, Cocteau explores the question of individuality versus mass society of which the life of the artist serves as a visible symbol. But since Cocteau's films, like Fellini's, for instance, are highly autobiographical, he uses himself as an example of the price to be paid for not toeing the line, as it were. Even though his early films can be considered surrealistic, the surrealists, both writers and film directors like Dali and Buñuel, criticized him for not being avant-garde enough. This accusation led Cocteau to a heated quarrel with Breton. In essence, *Blood of a Poet* is a testimony to the loneliness of the poet. After much exegesis of his work Cocteau became irritated when critics even went as far as to argue with him over the meaning and inspiration of his work. It was after such experiences that he wrote: "Poetry comes from those who are not concerned with it. We are cabinetmakers. The mediums come afterwards, and it is their business to make the tables talk."[1]

II

Orpheus (1950) is the middle film in the trilogy. This film is without a doubt the artistic and thematic pillar that anchors this ambitious trilogy. Stylistically, the film is a radical departure from the avant-garde mood of *Blood of a Poet*. *Orpheus* is the tale of a poet and the inwardly subjective struggle that he undergoes in order to be understood and respected outwardly, that is, objectively. The film is an existential trek through the life and suffering of a poet who is fated to come to terms with his destiny.

Cocteau's characterization of Orpheus as the protagonist of a poet/man of letters allows him to re-tell some rather universal and timeless truths using the voice of the present. The story begins with the narrator stating: "A privilege of a legend is to be without age." This statement is evidence that the Greek Orpheus and the mid-twentieth century French Orpheus is one and the same individual. They are both thinkers searching for the meaning of immortality.

The ancient legend presents Orpheus as a singer and animal charmer whose songs eventually distract him from paying due attention to his wife Eurydice. When the young woman dies, Orpheus is said to descend to hell where he charms its rulers and is therefore allowed to bring her back — on the condition that he does not look at her. Of course, this terrible binding condition is meant as a test to their love. When he does eventually look at her, she is torn apart by the Bacchantes or what were known to be the followers of the god Bacchus.

---

1. Professional Secrets: An Autobiography of Jean Cocteau. Translated from the French by Richard Howard. New York: Chilton Book Company, 1968. p.146.

Cocteau's Orpheus is a famous and highly-regarded poet who is envied and hated by his colleagues. Undoubtedly this autobiographical theme is a strong statement by Cocteau to his critics and detractors. This autobiographical theme is a central component of Cocteau's work. It is neither easy nor desirable to attempt to separate Cocteau's artistic vision from the fate of the poet in this trilogy.

The film begins as a crowd of writers is gathered at the Café des Poètes. This is the regular meeting place of the local literati. Orpheus is invited to sit in a table next to a sarcastic, though cordial, acquaintance. From the outset the man tells Orpheus, "Your gravest fault is knowing how far one can go before going too far." This is to be taken as a criticism that perhaps Orpheus is too seemingly rational to be truly free.

The drama of the story begins when a young poet is hit and killed by a pair of motorcycles outside the café. Death arrives quickly on the scene, and asks Orpheus to help her place Cegeste's body in her black Rolls Royce. Rather than taking him to a hospital, she takes Orpheus and the dead poet to her house in the underworld where she revives him in plain view of Orpheus. She answers Orpheus' protests by telling him, "You try too hard to understand and that is a mistake." The theme of understanding is very commonly found throughout Cocteau's work. This theme serves as a clear indication of the epistemological differences that Cocteau suggests exists between the nature of the poet and those valued by a positivistic age. He seems to express the Platonic notion that understanding and wisdom are not the same thing. While the scientist attempts to decode the function of physical and biological laws, the poet situates himself amidst these laws and ponders what such principles can mean to his existence. Orpheus' greater search for meaning is an exploration of human mortality, or immortality as the case may be.

Orpheus' initiation in the underworld leaves him puzzled as to the role of the two aforementioned poles of human existence. Death tells him that mortals are ill prepared to comprehend the logic of death and the many mysteries that are inherent in human life. She tells him not to be afraid as she takes him by the hand and walks him through the mirror out of the underworld and back to the world of mortals. The mirror acts as the link that unites the world of the living and the dead. But the mirror, Cocteau suggests, is also an external conscience that forces man to glance inward.

Orpheus later awakens in a sand pit confused and disoriented. Waiting nearby in the Rolls Royce is Heurtebise, the driver, who takes Orpheus to his waiting wife. This scene works to set up the interplay that exists between the two dimensions that Cocteau explores in this film. Orpheus' obsession now turns to trying to understand the messages that are conveyed from the underworld through the car's radio. He becomes convinced that to understand these cryptic messages is tantamount to opening up a new way of understanding human reality.

Cocteau's point is that this kind of search is precisely what the poetic sentiment and enterprise must convey. His contention is that the difference between the world of the poet as an active seeker of understanding and that of the passive onlooker is one of degree. However, the level of degree between these two viewpoints is in direct proportion to the understanding of the world that is attained by these two types of people.

After this episode, Death begins to take an interest in Orpheus' life. The contemplation of the underworld and its relation to the world of the living is made manifest when death brings Cegeste, the dead poet, back to life. She tells him that he will now work for her. The same thing occurs to Orpheus, because the work that she has in mind for him is no less than the work of the poet. In the film, Death visits Orpheus and keeps him under her watch. But also, one can argue that Death also works her understanding into the poet by serving as a muse. Her role is to awaken man to the mysteries of being which modern man has subdued with the insistence that only scientific knowledge is desirable. This is yet another central component of the plight of the poet. For this reason Cocteau begins the film by stating that the truth that myths convey is so important that they are relevant to all ages. Orpheus becomes the watchman for Death because Death has timeless knowledge to impart to man. At this point the metaphysical and theological perspective offered by Cocteau becomes complicated: Death becomes enamored with Orpheus. The narrator explains, "And that first night the death of Orpheus entered his room and watched him sleep." Each night thereafter, Death returned to his room.

When Eurydice dies, Heurtebise returns Orpheus to the underworld in order to allow him to see his wife one more time. As they enter the underworld through the mirror in the bedroom, Heurtebise tells Orpheus, "Look at mirrors all your life and you will see death at work." The suggestion here is that death is not an alien reality to man, but rather one that resides within life itself. At this point Heurtebise tells Orpheus that it is not necessary to understand, only to believe.

As they enter the underworld, Heurtebise tells Orpheus that, "Life is a long death and that the dead think that they are alive because this has become a habit for them." This somnambulist state of being is Cocteau's major criticism of post-modernity. Visiting the underworld allows Orpheus to fine-tune his poetic sensibility. This is why he is of the conviction that hidden in the radio messages there exits some greater and deeper meaning that is there to be harnessed by man.

The central episode in *Orpheus* is said to be the hasty and ill-advised tribunal, as we are soon to discover to which Orpheus must present himself. The tribunal is made up of Death herself and her assistant. The proceedings of the makeshift trial begin when Death asks Orpheus, "What do you mean by poet?" To this question Orpheus merely answers, "To write and not to be a writer." Cocteau expands on this question in an essay that is part of *Diary of an Unknown* tilted, "On a Way of Life," when he writes, "One is either judge or accused. The judge sits, the accused stands. Live on your feet."[1] Death tells Orpheus that she too must obey a higher authority. But Orpheus is not content to simply answer the tribunal, so in an act of metaphysical rebellion he decides that death owes him an explanation as well. Orpheus asks Death to tell him who gives the orders. Her answer implies some kind of not so benevolent cosmic logos: "He exists nowhere...some imagine he thinks of us... Others think he imagines us...others say he sleeps and that we are his dreams...his bad dreams."[1]

For their indiscretion, Death and her assistant are now brought before this higher authority and chastised for letting mortals in on these eternal secrets. The tribunal decides that Death was acting on her own accord and not on the cosmic principles that even death must abide by. The tribunal's verdict is twofold: 1) Death and her assistant are released on bail, and 2) Orpheus is released but he cannot look at his wife Eurydice.

Orpheus returns with Eurydice to their home and painfully begins to acquaint himself with these binding rules that he must now obey. For a while he is able to control his temptation and desire to look at Eurydice, but in one instant he catches a glimpse of her in the car's rear view mirror and she vanishes, presumably back into the world of the dead. Orpheus is later accosted by an envious and resentful mob of poets outside his home. This is the same group of poets who gather at the Café des Poètes and who despise him for apparently not being avant-garde enough. Their envy springs from his popularity with his readers. Envy and resentment are themes that Cocteau views as eternal and universal. The mob breaks down the front gate of his property and attacks him. He is shot and killed. He is reunited with Death once again. However, for this latest indiscretion, two policemen of the underworld take Death and her assistant Heurtebise away.

The film ends with a narration, which states, "The death of a poet requires a sacrifice to render him immortal." More over, right

---

1. *Diary of an Unknown.* p.209. We can relate this problem of the creative will to William Barrett's apt description of consciousness as : "...a whole of which I have no grasp and which I must now proceed, with much sweat and toil, to articulate in its details. If our consciousness could not be groping in this way, it would cease to be genuinely creative, and it could not then be the powerful instrument that it has been in shaping human history." See: Death of the Soul: From Descartes to the Computer. p. 166.

1. *Orpheus.* (Film).

before she is taken away Death tells Orpheus that, "Without will power we are cripples." Cocteau's handling of the poet as a seeker of self-knowledge and by implication of immortality is a testament to personal expression and the price that such convictions force the poet into paying. One of the earliest literary examples of this metaphysical rebellion, as Camus has referred to this sentiment, is witnessed in Socrates' search for immortality. The significance of this search, Cocteau's tells us, is not the search itself but rather the fact that this enterprise is often directed at universal principles that man may not be fully equipped to understand. Fate is one of these ancient themes. But for fate to enact any kind of influence over us it must first be something that one recognizes and that one is willing to embrace. This is precisely what Cocteau means by willing.

III

Testament of Orpheus (1959) is the final installment of the Orpheus trilogy. This work fuses together many self-referential elements contained in the prior two films. In this work an Eighteenth Century poet returns in modern times. The poet, once again, is none other than Orpheus. The film opens with narration by Cocteau himself, as is often the case in his films. Narrative is central to Cocteau's work because it is a very amenable manner of combining the visual structure of film with the lyrical nature of poetry. This opening statement serves to set the stage for Cocteau's exploration of the nature of poetry and the desire for a Nietzschean truth, which he refers to as being "A truth beyond truth" that is not easily grasped by post-modernity. The film begins with the following affirmation:

> It is the unique power of cinema to allow a great many people to dream the same dream together and to present illusion to us together as it were strict reality. It is, in short, an admirable vehicle for poetry. My film is nothing other than a striptease act gradually peeling away my body to reveal my naked soul. For there is a considerable audience eager for this truth beyond truth that will

one day become the sign of our times. This is the legacy of a poet to youth in which he always found support.[1]

This film does not have an easily decipherable linear plot. But one can make the argument that the strength of Cocteau's films is his regard and development of philosophical themes in a surrealistic manner. The predominant theme in this work is that the poet is always a soul who becomes lost in his own day and age. This, as well as Cocteau's notion that the work of art is a quasi pre-existing entity in its own right, demonstrates a strong attachment to Platonic thought. But this is an aesthetic notion that is readily found in the thought of many artists. This very same idea, for instance, is also found in Michelangelo's notion that within any block of marble is contained a sculpture that awaits its liberation by the artist. Nowhere is this Platonic theme more clear than in the latter's unfinished statues, especially in the apparent agony of the emerging figures in *Captives*. This aesthetic notion seems to imply that artistic inspiration paves its way by other than purely physical means. For Cocteau, as well, cosmic time and our self-conscious, subjective understanding of our place in it becomes a crucial point in the fabric of this film.

At the start of the film we see a young boy sitting at a desk when Orpheus, who is played by Cocteau, appears dressed in Louis XV clothing inquiring about the boy's dead father who was an architect. Later he reappears to a woman sitting on a bench, rocking an infant. Both the woman and the baby are startled at this apparition, and the woman drops the child. Later, he appears to a woman taking an elderly wheelchair-bound man for a stroll. The woman tells Orpheus that the professor cannot hear or speak to him, given that his mother dropped him on his head as an infant. These sequential visits to different people through diverse time periods clearly suggest a soul who has become lost in space and time. The boy who was thirteen years old when the poet first appeared to him is now a scientist, Orpheus travels back and forth

---

1. *Testament of Orpheus.*

through time; he appears again and again to the scientist throughout the film. The poet's main interest in the professor is that the latter has invented a bullet that travels faster than the speed of light. Orpheus hopes that perhaps if he is shot with this bullet, he will not have to return to his own time but will remain in the present. The scientist and the poet begin to talk about the aims and limits of scientific materialism, when the conversation focuses on a mutual acquaintance, a professor Langevin. The scientist says:

> Professor Langevin was naïve, like all scholars. Only the nine-teenth century could believe in exact sciences. He did not know that time obeys the same laws as space.[1]

A particularly magical scene takes place when Orpheus is shot with one of these bullets and begins to walk in slow motion, now dressed in contemporary clothing. Then, walking along a deserted road, he enters a gypsy camp where a large picture of a man is placed on a fire. The scene is then played backwards and the picture is seen un-burning. This is the point when the film becomes autobiographical. Cocteau, who up to now had been playing the role of Orpheus, the poet, now begins to play himself as a film director. He states, "From far off I recognized the photograph of Cegeste from the end of my film Orphée." This apparent subjective confusion gives credence to the notion of the poet as being a soul who becomes lost in his own time. But this is also significant in that *Testament of Orpheus* was to be his last film. Understood as such, one can make the case that this film serves as a retrospective testament to Cocteau's life and artistic vision.

Cegeste is the guide who leads him through the underworld in *Orpheus*. Taking Cegeste's picture and throwing it into the sea, so as not to become concerned with such matters once again, he nevertheless states: "Fate told me I was about to do something foolish by throwing the pieces of Cegeste's picture into the sea." This results in the immediate appearance of Cegeste, who comes alive out of the water like Botticelli's Venus. He carries a hibiscus

---

1. *Testament of Orpheus.*

blossom, which he gives to Orpheus. From this point on the hibiscus flower becomes a symbol of rebirth, one resembling the phoenix.

Cegeste proceeds to guide Cocteau past a contest where a little girl is on a stage describing a Cocteau painting, while a judge tells her that Cocteau plays an artist. In other words, this is an allusion to Orpheus/Cocteau the poet as he comes to understand himself as an artist. He writes: "Naturally works of art create themselves and dream of killing their creators. Of course they exist before the artist discovers them. But it's always Orpheus, always Orpheus." By "killing their creators" he merely means that the work of art forces the artist to have to explain his work to the world-at-large.

Cegeste then decides to take him to the goddess whom some call Pallas Athene and others Minerva. When they arrive, Orpheus is taken before a tribunal where he is accused of two crimes: innocence, which essentially has to do with "being capable and culpable of all crimes rather than one in particular"; and "repeatedly attempting to trespass in another world." Cocteau pleads guilty to both crimes. He adds: "I am besieged by crimes I have not committed and have often been tempted to scale that mysterious fourth wall on which men inscribe their loves and their dreams." This fourth wall is no doubt an allusion to the fourth dimension or what has to do with the nature of time itself.

"But why is this?" the two members of the tribunal ask. To this he answers, "World weary, perhaps, and a hatred of habit. Defiance of the rules...that creativity which is the highest form of humanity's spirit of contradiction." This segment of the film serves as an autobiographical settling of the score with Cocteau's critics, as it were. The tribunal then asks him, "What then do you mean by film?" "A film," he answers, "is a petrifying fountain of thought. A film reviews lifeless deeds. A film permits one to give the appearance of reality to that which is unreal." They then continue their analytical assault by asking him, "What do you mean by unreal?" To which he answers, "That which lies beyond our meager limits." Of course, the tribunal works as a form of chastisement and not as an honest appeal to truth.

146

"What, then, is a poet?" they continue. The poet answers, "In creating poems, the poet uses a language neither living nor dead spoken by few and understood by few." They then go on to ask whether such language is necessary at all. Now, realizing that they already possess the answers which they seek in him, he can no longer hold back and answers, "To contact their like in a world where the exhibitionism of boring the soul is usually practiced by the blind." The tribunal is a preventive measure or so the judges claim, whose purpose is to prevent the poet from becoming too distracted from mortal concerns. They tell him that the worst punishment for a poet would be to live in between two worlds or what a film director would call in "false contrast." The tribunal condemns him "to live" and sends him off. In a satirical vein that is aimed at both post-modernity as well as his critics, Cocteau asks Cegeste, "What is this statue that eats autographs?" To this the young poet answers: "It is the instant celebrity machine. Fame for anyone in a minute or two. Beyond that, of course, it becomes more difficult. In developed countries the workday is short." This is clearly a refutation of that celebrity seeking impulse, which Cocteau's ascribes to false prophets and artists. Cocteau forcibly drives this point home by further asking? "What is coming from its mouth?" "Novels, poems, songs and so forth. It stops until it's fed by new autograph hunters. The rest of the time, it digests, ponders, sleeps."[1]

He then enters some ruins where two horses and some men are waiting for him. One of the men throws a lance through him that impales him to the ground. This is one more allusion to the judging eye and scrutiny of the critics.

In a very significant scene, his blood and the hibiscus flower that he carries throughout the film turn red. This is Cocteau's only use of color in the three films. This seems to beg the question whether Orpheus' life is a testament to reality or illusion. While he is resting on a bed the gypsies begin to sing him a lament, at which

---

1. *Testament of Orpheus.*

point he comes back to life as Oedipus. He says, "Pretend to weep, my friends, since poets only pretend to die." He then goes on to say, "The sphinx, Oedipus, those whom one is so eager to meet, you may one day meet them and yet not see them." The autobiographical narrator then closes the scene by saying:

> So there you are. A wave of joy has carried away my farewell film. I will be sad if you did not like it because I gave it my all, as much as any member of my crew. My star is a Hibiscus flower. Any celebrities you may have recognized along the way appear not because they are famous but because they are the roles they play and because they are my friends.[1]

The convincing stature of Cocteau's philosophical and aesthetic vision is not found solely in these three films. On the contrary, his films are an exceptional example of a thinker personifying metaphysical reflection in a visual and differentiated narrative. I would argue that his films are only an empirical attempt to establish the urgency of an appeal to existential human essence. Cocteau's cinematic works are an offshoot of the overall philosophical project that he showcases in his written work. It is for this reason that his films have been criticized as too highbrow. But his themes are none other than those that philosophers have always employed. It seems ironic that, because cinema serves as a mirror to human existence, such themes should be rejected when employed in a visual medium.

---

1. *Testament of Orpheus.*

CHAPTER 7. CAMUS' HERO OF THE ABSURD

> When I was young, I asked more of people than they
> could give: everlasting friendship, endless feeling.
> Now I know to ask less of them than they can give: a
> straightforward companionship. And their feelings,
> their friendship, their generous actions seem in my
> eyes to be wholly miraculous: a consequence of grace
> alone. — Albert Camus

Albert Camus died in an automobile accident on January 4,
1960, on the Nationale 5 road. He was carrying with him an
unfinished novel titled *The First Man (Le Premier Homme)*. The novel is
an autobiographical work. The circumstances surrounding his death
at the age of forty-six might be considered the closing of what
Camus referred to as an absurd existence. Even though this novel is
incomplete, *The First Man* leaves an invaluable indication as to
precisely what the major philosophical themes of this work were to
be. Camus had compiled a series of "notes" and "sketches" that were
to serve as a working outline for the novel, including entire lines of
dialogue, some substantial enough to give a clear understanding as

to the time, characters and literary voice in this work. This novel was published in 1994 under the direction of Camus' two children. As his daughter relates, in the editor's note that appears at the beginning of the book, Camus would have never agreed to publish an unfinished novel. However, the novel was developed far along enough to merit a qualified publication. The reception of this conditional publication by a major twentieth-century thinker would undoubtedly depend on the good will of the critics. This seems a timely and fundamental fact given that Camus' life and work were seriously hampered by the caustic will of ideological nay-sayers.

Because *The First Man* is autobiographical and because Camus' thought always revolves around the autonomy of the individual in what he deems as an objectifying cosmos, I believe that these notes serve an even more important and poignant role in his exploration of individuality. A philosophical perspective that frames and attempts to differentiate the existence of his characters informs all of Camus' literary creation. For this reason, I will argue that *The First Man* leaves the reader, if not the Camus scholar, in a very rare and even unique position. In this work, which from all indications was to be a much longer work than the published 281 pages, Camus was intent on writing a literary autobiography. Throughout the notes he offers a glimpse into the indignation that he felt for those who are too quick to judge a work of art without due regard for its author. The notes and sketches leave the reader with a clearer and more intimate picture of the private Camus. Artistic creation and the vital trajectory of the thinker cannot be easily separated.

The publication of this work also served as a test of good will between those whose vocation it is to create and those whose mode of making a living is to impart criticism. Unfortunately, regardless of questions of technical conventions and literary merit, a great part of literary debates and disputes can be viewed as an objectifying and blind disregard for human autonomy. Yet thinking and writing can be a rather tenuous business because concerns for human freedom, individuality, and existential autonomy always find their way into all of Camus' work.

There are very striking philosophical similarities between *The First Man* and Camus' first book, *A Happy Death*, for instance. In *A Happy Death*, which he completed in 1938 at the age of twenty-five, the author develops a very interesting, if not altogether original, idea of the thinker attempting to capture the essence and immediacy of death itself. In this work the young Camus is concerned with living a good life in order to have a "happy" death. In other words, Camus' main contention has everything to do with Socrates' notion that all philosophy is a preparation for death through a conscious readiness to die. *A Happy Death* is essentially a meditation on the values of a future oriented existence that is aware that the future is already imbedded in a vitally lived immediacy. The theme of the passage of time is a central and unifying theme in these two works. In *A Happy Death* Patrice Mersault, the autobiographical main character, comes to the realization that to possess time can be both magnificent and very dangerous. The rallying point of this contention is that idleness is a fatal condition to existential stagnation and mediocrity. However, this, he tells us, cannot be said of the creative life. Instead, Camus argues that true reflection can only exist when framed by the presence of idle time. In *The First Man* Camus follows through with this same concern. The death of his father in the latter work signifies the horror that the passage of time can mean to a reflective soul. Mersault and Jacques desire transcendence, one that will round out their lives. In both cases, the consensus is that happiness originates from having a pure heart and the necessary will to implement the virtues thereof.

Camus' situation as a philosopher and writer is a rather precarious one. There is a sense in which he can easily be regarded as a stoic. His notion of metaphysical rebellion showcases a courageous engagement with reality that leaves no room for external blame or sentimental rationalization. In addition, he does not allow this frustrated metaphysical rebellion the indiscretion of becoming the basis and escape valve of ideology. But stoics usually shun the world of men and retire to a private existence. Camus clearly does not take this route as is evident from his engagement in the French resistance and his concern for the plight of those living under the rigors of the Soviet Union. However, there is a also a very reserved and dignified side to Camus the man, which he found to be at odds with Camus the public entity. He seems to have found a resolute answer to this dilemma by demanding that the autonomy of the thinker as one who attempts to bring coherence to what Kant has called the "chaos of sensations" is respected. The thinker for Camus is always a creator of worlds. A very strong indication of the respect that he felt for other thinkers and the creative process itself is seen in the scant number of negative references that he makes in reference to the work of others. In *The Myth of Sisyphus*, Camus does make mention of Dostoyevsky, when he writes of *The Brothers Karamazov* and Kafka's *The Trial* and *The Castle*, but he always does so in a positive light. His references to Nietzsche, Kierkegaard and Chestov are instances of praise that allow Camus to argue a particular point. The rest of *The Myth of Sisyphus* is an exploration of the nature of life and death and the Socratic question of what constitutes a worthwhile life. Equally true, in *The Rebel* Camus stirs clear of offhanded criticism of the thought of others. In the first part of that work the focus is on man's place in what he considers an absurd universe. The first part of *The Rebel* is reminiscent of the vital and intellectual sincerity of the thought of such thinkers as Marcus Aurelius, Kierkegaard and Nietzsche, to mention just a few. The second part of this book offers a criticism of the tyrannical consequences that Marxism wrought on Soviet bloc nations. This part of the work offers an indictment of ideology and how this subsumes life itself to the state. This section of the work is comparable to Czeslaw Milosz's *The Captive Mind* and Ortega's *The Revolt of the Masses* in its ability to pinpoint how existential malcontentment leads to public tyranny. To his critics, we must point out that time has vindicated Camus in his understanding of these historic facts. In opposition to Sartre's extensive emphasis on dialectical materialism, Camus demonstrates great foresight in his understanding that it is the dialectic of the lived experience which is the true foundation of history. This latter insight, Camus aptly discovers, is based on the exigencies of human reality and not necessarily on social-political expediency.

In the autobiographical novel, the author possesses an added direction and vision to his work that the reader may neither suspect or that he is privy to. Most philosophical works have traditionally excluded concern for the thinker as an autonomous being. Perhaps this is perfectly appropriate given the complexities and rigor involved in works of philosophy. But this is neither completely necessary or is it true in many cases. Camus' work demonstrates a detailed and accomplished acumen for existentially vital concerns that speak to the conscientious reader. It would seem inappropriate and even asinine to treat such questions in the clinical and detached manner that positivist philosophers have so often undertaken. This personal and autobiographical stake in a work of literature is an aspect of the creative process that ought to be immune from the ire of the critic.

Still more important, *The First Man* enables the discerning reader the ability to look into the formative stages of the creative vision itself. This is a telling and insightful glimpse into the creative process due to the autonomous privacy that only the author can enjoy. Consider Nabokov's notion that only fools or novices show their unfinished work to others. But the creative process is much more than forging a sketch of a future work. This process involves an aesthetic and moral vision that must revolve around the vital concerns of the thinker as a person. Strictly speaking, the dichotomous nature of the will and vision of the thinker cannot be reconciled by the critic without doing so in the terms that the thinker has set for himself. This standstill is a clear-cut example of the hazards that reflection provides, especially under conditions where the knowledge in question is of a vital-existential kind. These concerns are clearly discernable in these notes and sketches. This is the case because in these notes Camus works out the specific details and vital makeup of the world that he was intent on describing.

Amongst the main themes found in *The First Man*, at least three can be easily isolated: 1) What he called a "Robert Musil theme": the search for salvation of the soul in the modern world, 2) The isolation that the writer/thinker must bear, and 3) The search for individual autonomy.[1]

Camus' reference to Robert Musil presumably alludes to the latter's novel, *The Man Without Qualities*. This reference questions the possibility of arriving at meaning in the modern world. One of Camus' fundamental presuppositions for asking this question has to do with Nietzsche's assertion that God is dead. If the notion that God is dead is accepted, then everyone finds himself burdened with the responsibility of fashioning existence alone. The other has to do with the dehumanizing and objectifying force that lies at the center of the modern state. The totalitarian state, especially the Soviet model, Camus viewed as eliminating any possibility for true hope and genuine peace.

The Man Without Qualities is part of the wealth of European literature that came forth during the very fertile inter-war period (between World War I and II). Even though Musil's extensive novel technically limits its plot to concentration on the anticipation of the First World War, he is still concerned with the isolation of the individual in modern society. Both the search for meaning and the salvation of the soul in the modern world are equally recurring themes throughout all of Camus' work.

In "Pessimism and Courage," an essay contained in his book *Resistance, Rebellion and Death*, he takes up this same point. Camus writes:

---

1. *The First Man* is an autobiographical novel. The main character in this work is Jacques Cormery, a young boy. Through Jacques Camus reflects on his childhood in Algeria, his love for his mother and the ever-present Camus depiction of the sun. See: Robert Musil's *Man Without Qualities*. Translated by Sophie Wilkins. New York: Vintage International, 1996. This unfinished novel is a tour de force that deals with the two years (1913-1914) in the life of the main character named Ulrich. The novel is a study of the days leading up to WWI as Ulrich turns his back on morality and all conventions. The novel is in effect a close look at the rising tide of nihilism in the west.

We want to think and live in our history. We believe that the truth of this age can be found only by living through the drama of it to the very end. If the epoch has suffered from nihilism, we cannot remain ignorant of nihilism and still achieve the moral code we need. No, everything is not summed up in negation and absurdity. We know this. But we must first posit negation and absurdity because they are what our generation has encountered and what we must take into account.[1]

But this condition of exile that Camus feels is not to be confused with alienation in the sense that Sartre uses this word. One who feels himself alienated from others, a particular society or institution, for instance, has the hope of coming out of this loneliness or longing for a union with the source of his alienation. But this is not Camus' main line of reflection because alienation more often than not is described as a diffuse feeling of withdrawal or "nausea" from things commonly shared. Exile for Camus served the author to signify the existence of a permanent wall that separates man from any true penetration into the mystery of life and death. The question of exile for Camus can be construed to exhibit several possible meanings. One of these is the literal exile that he lived in being away from his home in Algeria. Camus is also a fine example of the Mediterranean temperament. His novels are replete with reverence for the sun and its effects on the Algerian people and their way of life. He embraced the French, that is, the European manner of life without seemingly abandoning his love of his Algerian upbringing. This question of the relationship of philosophy to temperament is one that is brilliantly taken up by Ortega y Gasset as well as Julián Marías among others. Camus brings up this point in *Notebooks 1935-1942*, where he mentions that every philosophy is a direct example of a respective thinker. But exile also means Camus' understanding that the ontological and fundamental condition of man is always to live one's life alone. Another notion of exile has to do with Camus' concern for the uniqueness and thus irreducible quality of the circumstances that each individual must bear. In many

---

1. *The First Man*, p. 59.

respects Camus' work can be liken to an aesthetic of life. He is a philosopher with a singular vision of what life means to those who reflect on both, its depravities as well as its glory.

When Jacques Cormery, the autobiographical forty-year old main character of *The First Man* goes in search of his father's tomb what Camus depicts is nothing other than a stoic attitude toward life. In some absolutely stunningly beautiful passages Camus' narrator reflects on the passage of time and what this all means to subjectivity. Upon realizing that his father, who died in World War I, was only twenty-nine years of age, the narrator writes of Jacques' encounter with time:

> The course of time itself was shattering around him while he remained motionless among those tombs he now no longer saw, and the years no longer kept to their places in the great river that flows to its end.[1]

At this point Jacques not only begins to mourn the death of his father at such an early age, but he also confronts his own history and how the years have already robbed him of half of his life. Jacques' exile from "the deadly order of the world" pins him against an alien world from which thought offers no respite.[2] This passage is a supreme example of Camus' firm grasp and clear exposition of existential concerns. Philosophically speaking, this is what Jaspers means by saying that my existence is never an object for me, but rather a reality that I must live from within. In exercising our freedom to live we remain in search of our essence as this is symbolized by all of our actions. However, by over intellectualizing this process what we end up with is nothing other than an abstract concept. Camus also saw that existential categories could not be intellectualized without simultaneously robbing them of their immediate reality. Jacques' arrival at the understanding that his life will always be a transparent phenomenon and thus never an object of thought makes him appreciate the vital categories of existence

---

1. Ibid., p. 26.
2. Ibid., p. 26.

evermore. This fascination with the concept of time and how this fluid reality frames human existence is already present in *The Happy Death*, his first novel. But the aforementioned passage also shows the respect that Camus had for the destiny of the individual as a concrete cosmic entity. The sense of the absurd that man feels, Camus argues, ought to become directed to life itself given the limitations of man's essential metaphysical condition. Thus Camus' notion of revolt is always aimed at the absurdity that the cosmos represents and which cannot be subdued through rational thought. This is the same outrage and indignation that is felt by Gilgamesh on the death of his best friend Enkidu. The greatest of human contemplative problems for Camus always have to do with the question of mortality. But this metaphysical outrage is fortuitously transformed and elevated into an appreciation of the sublime. For this reason his treatment of subjectivity and individuality always grapple with the fate of man as he appears on the scene and in the only manner in which man must live: alone.

After Jacques' initial shock at the realization that he has now outlived his father by eleven years, it dawns on him that what separates the living from the dead is time, a relentless mystery that ossifies all human existence into non-being. The narrator explains:

> But, in the strange dizziness of that moment, the statue every man eventually erects and that hardens in the fire of the years, into which he then creeps and there awaits its final crumbling — that statue was rapidly cracking, it was already collapsing.[1]

To attempt to extract a ready-made epistemology from these vital moments is not only an exercise in intellectual futility, but it is also to rob life of its immediacy. Some critics have condemned Camus' thought to exist solely on a literary plain. In essence this manner of "demoting" his contribution to philosophical thought by only attributing to it a literary value misses the point of his thought altogether. Camus' philosophy, like that of other similar writers such as Nietzsche, Kierkegaard, Unamuno and Kafka, for instance,

---

1. Ibid., p. 26.

is centered around the encounter of the individual with the cosmos, and not necessarily with an attempt to amplify such findings for all men. Such criticism of his thought, of course, is ludicrous given the existential themes that he was concerned with. Camus' respect for individuality and personal autonomy came at a time in history when these notions were first being attacked from many quarters. In European philosophy at that time, the dominant voice was the fervor that materialism, especially positivism and analytic philosophy had fomented. In America, pragmatism was all the rage. Of course, Marxism and its many variants denied the possibility of any personal transcendence. The entire spectrum of Camus' writing was precisely a reaction to these objectifying forces.

Also, to this kind of criticism we can argue that Camus' main objective was to explicate what it meant for him to live. Some critics are moved by the dangerous assumption that philosophy per se can only come about through the genre of the philosophical treatise. But to Camus' credit, we can see that he denies that philosophical problems must be addressed in any fixed philosophical forum. What he suggests instead is that thinkers ought not to become limited by the explication of formal problems. This incessant attempt to separate Camus from his philosophy, which is due in part to his alleged "misreading" of Hegel, further demonstrates the differences between a genuine philosophizing and mere criticism. Camus' philosophical and literary output is a vital overflow of his life and circumstances. This is not a mere historicism, but an understanding that existential thought is also always biographical in nature. But if these are not the true conditions and background of all genuine reflection, then clearly philosophy today has been subsumed by a new form of scholasticism. Camus' conception of philosophical reflection is akin to that of a pair of crutches or a compass, that is — philosophy is conceived as an aide to help us navigate through existence. All movements that have attempted to locate the essence of man in collective structures have always done so by undermining the individual. This is a criticism that Camus feels at ease in pointing out in both the modern state and religion.

These are precisely some of the very forces that Camus fought against with his life and work.

The First Man is a unique example of the artistic process in full blossom as well as the natural dialectic that informs all reflection. Many writers have left notes that accompany their published work, but few of these have been unfinished works. And even fewer still are the notes of a gifted thinker on the verge of synthesizing a worldview. However, the notes and sketches that pertain to *The First Man* ought not to be confused with his two *Notebooks* that are dated 1935-1942 and 1942-1951 respectively. These two works contain overall notes, ideas and even short essays, but they do not make up the outline of any specific work. For this reason, the importance of *The First Man* cannot be viewed in isolation, but rather as a corollary to his other works and his development as a philosopher.

Another important theme that this novel develops is that of the loneliness of the writer. Writers, of course, do not monopolize loneliness. Loneliness is a central component in the role that subjectivity plays in human existence. But Camus was very concerned with loneliness from a very early age. In *Notebooks: 1935-1942* he contrasts the loneliness that is found in the city with that of the desert, for instance. There he refers to the city, and Paris specifically as the last desert. And when Camus writes in his notes that the nobility of the writer's occupation always lies in resisting oppression, hence in accepting isolation he is equating writing with moral courage and aesthetic vision. Oppression for Camus is both metaphysical and social-political. The interesting irony of his particular circumstances is that the very same ideological forces that were incapable of making sense of the absurd were also the ones who sidetracked his career. For this reason he chose to talk about the loneliness of the ancient Greek thinker, Empedocles. Empedocles is a suitable source of inspiration for Camus due to the latter's understanding of the universe as a battleground of conflicting and thus opposing forces. The strife that lies at the center of Empedocles' thought is also Camus' notion of the conflict that man must attempt to settle between his existential condition and the cosmically objectifying. His answer to this existential dilemma is solved through his love and thus acceptance of life and his repudiation of politics as a form of power struggle. Another one of the ironies in Camus' later life is that his major form of loneliness was dealt to him by the spite of ideologues in their quest for the exercise of power.

Camus was pilloried by his peers for his criticism of the Soviet Union and the attack on autonomy and individuality that Stalinism represented. His position was not politically correct among leftist thinkers at the time. But Camus was not alone in condemning the Soviet system. Czeslaw Milosz's book *The Captive Mind* (1953) paints a historically accurate, moral and psychological picture of the ideological character type that created and operated the early forms of repression.[1] Solzhenitsyn, Orwell and Koestler amongst many others have also written insightful testimonies to such violations of human autonomy. To ignore and criticize such testimonies demonstrates the objectifying and anti-humanitarian fervor that infused some leftist intellectuals dating back to the 1920s. The astonishing degree of this ill will can be seen even after Camus fought the Nazis as part of the French resistance during the German occupation, and opposed Franco's government. In the eyes of his leftist critics, Camus' crime was twofold: 1) he renounced his membership in the communist party at a time when this action

---

1. Czeslaw Milosz wrote, in *To Begin Where I Am: Collected Essays*, that Albert Camus was a modern-day Cathar. This is a considerable argument, especially when we take a close look at the overall tone of *The First Man*. Milosz as well as other critics has speculated that perhaps Camus was beginning to soften up his views on God and the absurd at the time of his death. Milosz writes: "The first work by Camus was his university dissertation on St. Augustine. Camus, in my opinion, was also a Cathar, a pure one, and if he rejected God it was out of love for God because he was not able to justify him. The last novel written by Camus, *The Fall*, is nothing else but a treatise on grace — absent grace — though it is also a satire: the talkative hero, Jean Baptiste Clamence, who reverses the words of Jesus and instead of "Judge not and ye shall not be judged" gives the advice "Judge, and ye shall not be judged," could be, I have reason to suspect, Jean-Paul Sartre." Another reason that Milosz holds this view has to do with what he considers Camus' view that history is a battleground for good and evil. p. 253.

could do the most damage to it, and 2) he verbalized his dismay over Soviet excesses. It would seem to humanists that this second move on Camus' part demonstrated a "commitment" to the truth. Instead, to ideologues the reality of this second crime meant the weakening of the Marxist theoretical position regardless of the verifiable facts. This latter fact is at the center of Camus' falling out with Sartre. For these two acts of valor Camus was never forgiven. It is this, in large measure, that Camus refers to when he mentions the isolation of the writer. He simply became a pariah. An indication of this sentiment can be seen in what the narrator of *The First Man* has to say of Jacques' friend Malan:

> Yet he was immensely cultivated and J.C. admired him unre-
> servedly, for Malan, in a day when outstanding men are so banal,
> was the one person who had his own way of thinking, to the
> extent that that is possible. At any rate, under his deceptively
> accommodating exterior, he was free and uncompromisingly orig-
> inal in his opinions.[1]

Another point that makes Camus' moral courage even more commendable is the poverty from which he arose in his native Algeria and from which he eventually lifted himself. That leftist intellectuals, most whom were bourgeois themselves, should ignore and downplay this fact demonstrates the daunting degree to which ideology will go in negating the autonomy of the individual. Having been brought up by his mother after his father was killed during World War I, still managed to achieve a degree of dignity that refused poverty as a permanent condition. In this respect Camus can be seen as a working class hero. He represents the ideal of the democratic process where the plight of the individual is left to its own autonomous devices.

He also developed a strong sense of pride in remembering those who helped him. Camus' sense of loyalty is always a central aspect of his thought. This may be in keeping with his stoic and classical

---

1. Ibid., p.30.

notion of honor. William Barrett, a thinker whose authoritative books on existentialism have always proven to be on the mark, writes in *Time of Need*:

> From the experimentation in form and language that has been one of the hallmarks of modern literature, Camus remained aloof, deliberately pursuing a kind of classicism that takes us back, beyond the realistic novel of the nineteenth, to the recit, the short moralizing tale, of the eighteenth century. [1]

This classical respect for honor is displayed throughout *The First Man*. When Jacques Cormery is talking to his friend Malan, he thanks him for helping him rise above his poverty. Jacques says:

> When I was very young, very foolish, and very much alone — you remember, in Algiers? — You paid attention to me and, without seeming to, you opened for me the door to everything I love in the world. [2]

And when Malan responds by saying that Cormery was gifted, Jacques immediately makes him understand that natural talent is often not enough for success. This is also in keeping with Camus' equation of freedom with limitation. Jacques tells Malan:

> Of course. But even the most gifted person needs someone to initiate him. The one that life puts in your path one day, that person must be loved and respected forever, even if he's not responsible. That is my faith. [3]

This sense of loyalty is a reaction to the adversity that poverty had put Camus through and which he refused to convert into the fuel of ideology. After his break with the communist party Camus saw himself as not easily belonging or identifying with any particular group. It is interesting to note that Camus was always marred by the loneliness of this metaphysical exile. Following the

1. William Barrett. *Time of Need: Forms of Imagination in the Twentieth Century.* New York: Harper & Row Publishers, 1972, p. 28.
2. *The First Man*, p.33.
3. Ibid.

notes to *The First Man*, the editors inserted two letters that Camus wrote to Monsieur Germain, his grade school teacher in Algiers. One letter was dated November 19, 1957 and offers a heartfelt appreciation for his old teacher because, as Camus writes:

> Without you, without the affectionate hand you extended to the small poor child that I was, without your teaching, and your example, none of all this would have happened.[1]

In the letter he mentions that, after receiving the news that he had won the Nobel Prize, he first thought of his mother and then of Monsieur Germain. This is the kind of undying loyalty to individual autonomy that cannot occur in the mind of the ideologue due to the privileged position that it attributes to politics. It is also a fine example of the serious devotion that Camus felt toward concrete individuals. Barrett writes:

> But the trouble is that the professional revolutionary is apt to become the servitor of his ideas rather than their master and consequently he is led to set his abstractions above the processes of life itself, and in their name to murder, if need be, millions of people.[2]

But for Camus this sense of loyalty does not end with people. Camus felt a keen desire to keep the memory of the ancient Greeks alive as well. His devotion to universal beauty serves as a repudiation of what he considered to be the tortured and aimless art of modern man. In retrospect we can see that Barrett correctly sums up Camus' basic moral and artistic orientation toward modernity when he writes of Camus' essay, "Helen's Exile":

> Helen is the ancient symbol of human beauty, and modern artists, in Camus' view, have exiled her from our midst to pursue an art of tortured expressionism.[3]

---

1. Ibid., p. 321.
2. *Time of Need*, p. 48.
3. Ibid., p.28.

This cultural and artistic alienation is yet another form that exile signifies for him. Camus testifies to this himself in his notes when he writes:

> What has helped me bear an adverse fate will perhaps help me accept an overly favorable outcome — and what has most sustained me was the great vision, the very great vision I have of art.[1]

Part of this vision was the realization that human life was the greatest work of art for him. This joie de vivre that his work exudes is a negation of the rampant nihilism that he witnessed in most of contemporary philosophy and literature. He alludes to this point in the notes by saying:

> One cannot live with truth — "knowingly" —, he who does so sets himself apart from other men, he can no longer in any way share their illusion. He is an alien — and that is what I am.[2]

Camus' notion of man in revolt, much like Ortega's "I and my circumstances" is a confrontation between man and the cosmos. The comparison between these two thinkers should not go unnoticed because Camus had great reverence for Ortega, even once referring to him as one of the greatest European thinkers after Nietzsche. Also, both of these thinkers refused to allow their thought to become subsumed by ideology or politics. In *The Revolt of the Masses* Ortega argued that politics always remains as the lowest rung of all civilizations and cultures. The reason for this is because Ortega realized that most political problems are always metaphysical/moral problems that merely bubble up to the surface in what some would consider political ways.

The task that Camus issues for Sisyphus is one where man lives on without the hope of transcendence. Again, in the notes to *The First Man* Camus earmarks this theme by writing: "Finally he takes

---

1. *The First Man*, p. 320.
2. Ibid., p. 295.

Empedocles as his model. The philosopher who lives alone."[1] This stoic ideal and resignation, then, far from being construed as defeatist becomes for Camus the rallying cry for embracing life. Camus' zest for life is founded on the principle that life is irreplaceable and irreducible to any abstraction. He emphasized that life — even with all of its difficulties was his only faith.

It is correct to say that Camus' thought can be fundamentally divided into two periods: 1) that of the *Myth of Sisyphus*, and 2) *The Rebel*. But it is also correct to assume that his notion of revolt and exile was only exacerbated through the injustice that he received at the hands of ideological critics. This fact is easily ascertained in *The First Man*.

In a poignant note of indignation and resignation to his fate he has Jacques say:

> I've lived too long, and acted and felt, to say this one is right and that one wrong. I've had enough of living according to the image others show me of myself. I'm resolved on autonomy, I demand independence in interdependence.[2]

A stark example of the excessive criticism and personal attacks that he underwent is found in the unbalanced and apologist book by Patrick McCarthy, *Camus*. Unlike the sensitive and truth seeking works on Camus by William Barrett; the insightful *Albert Camus of Europe and Africa* (1970) by Conor Cruise O'Brien; and the two excellent works by Germaine Brée titled *Camus* (1959) and *Camus and Sartre: Crisis and Commitment* (1972), McCarthy makes an ideological mockery of Camus' thought.

McCarthy writes in 1976 about Camus' cosmic indignity or Revolt:

> Man is still balanced on a tightrope between his sense of the sacred and his awareness that he must die and revolt is still a demand for unity, which the world cannot answer. It is a negative

---

1. Ibid., p. 309.
2. Ibid., p. 292.

trait, a creature of division and stoical contemplation. It cannot construct values, which would dissolve the skepticism that is one of its components. Its chief characteristic is that it refuses the leap of faith which revolution represents.[1]

McCarthy's criticism is high-flown and oozes with injustice because Camus' main point in *The Rebel* is precisely to demonstrate that the existential problems of man, as a cosmic being cannot be assuaged by political solutions. McCarthy's criticism is purely political and as such it presupposes that all thought ought to be guided toward a political dimension. But this is precisely where this logic goes wrong. At end of the second part of *The Rebel* the author offers an analysis of how, after one hundred and fifty years of nihilism, metaphysical revolt has given way to state sponsored terror. But then, to point this out is one of those alleged indecencies for which the left will not forgive Camus. Furthermore, to call Camus a "creature of stoical contemplation" is to distort the independent nature of what it means to be a stoic. Again, McCarthy's dogmatically ideological position is to convert all thought into praxis. But what he has in mind is not just any praxis, rather one that is oriented toward political means. On the contrary, Camus' vision as a thinker begins with his vital suffering as an autonomous being. Perhaps what Mr. McCarthy argued for was a "commitment" to political praxis, one that is capable of changing the order of social/political reality. But if "commitment" is what ideological critics demanded of Camus, all they had to do was listen in good will to what he had been saying, dating back to his commentaries in *Combat*. Furthermore, Camus understood that to change the political status quo was not to answer the vital/existential questions of life itself such as, for example, the question of human mortality. And, for Mr. McCarthy to write the following, at such a late date as 1982:

1. Patrick McCarthy. *Camus*. New York: Random House, 1982, p. 251.

While spending hundreds of pages attacking Marxism Camus offers few alternative forms of protest. This robs his book of diversity and turns it into even more of a lament.[1]

Again, the audacity to make such a claim can only be founded on intellectual hypocrisy. Camus and many other Western intellectuals already knew in the 1930s and certainly in the 1940s that the Soviet system had an array of fellow travelers, allies and mouthpieces in the West that were quick to voice their propagandistic concerns on demand. Where were the humanistic concerns of these intellectuals? And as for the charge that Camus makes "few alternative forms of protest," it seems self-serving and ingenious because Mr. McCarthy's fallacious logic implies that Soviet totalitarianism was the solution to the inherent problems of Western democracies and capitalism. Apparently Camus' spirited protest at the crimes of the totalitarian state was simply not welcome.

In contradistinction to McCarthy's caustic invective, Lev Braun's brilliant analysis, *Witness of Decline, Albert Camus: Moralist of the Absurd* more accurately depicts Camus' historical clarity in his portentous understanding of the nature of the totalitarian state. Braun cites the humanitarianism in Camus' insightful article on the terrors of Hungarian socialist totalitarianism.

> For it is indeed a counter-revolutionary state. What else can we call a regime that forces the father to inform on his son, the son to demand the supreme punishment for his father, the wife to bear witness against her husband — that has raised denunciation to the level of a virtue? Foreign tanks, police, twenty-year-old girls hanged, committees of workers decapitated and gagged, scaffolds, writers departed and inspired, the lying press, camps, censorship, judges arrested, criminals legislating, and the scaffold again — is this socialism, the great celebration of liberty and justice?
>
> No, we have known, we still know this kind of thing; these are the bloody and monstrous rites of the totalitarian religion! Hun-

---

1. Ibid., p. 251.

garian socialism is in prison or in exile today. In the palaces of the state, armed to the teeth, slink the belly tyrants of absolutism.[1]

One must remember that Camus' humanism was a genuine desire to improve or at worst keep man's existential condition from worsening. Also, it is important to keep in mind that the author of the aforementioned was the same thinker who, as Braun explains, "resigned his post in UNESCO in 1952 to protest Franco's Spain's admission."[2]

The personal autonomy that Camus demonstrates can be equated with the singular aesthetic vision and moral courage that he was to outline later in *The First Man*. In spite of McCarthy's call for an "alternative" to Marxism, Camus had indeed already offered an old alternative to terror: liberty. In "Socialism of the Gallows," Camus makes it clear in no uncertain terms that true heroism demands a desire for freedom from all quarters. In this essay he challenges intellectuals to understand that ideas, both good and bad, can have serious consequences. He explains:

> But first our leftist intellectuals, who have swallowed so many many insults and may well have to begin doing so again, would have to undertake a critique of the reasoning and ideologies to which they have hitherto subscribed, which have wreaked the havoc they have seen in our most recent history. That will be the hardest thing. We admit that today conformity in on the left. To be sure, the right is not brilliant, but the left is in complete decadence, a prisoner of words, caught in its own vocabulary, capable merely of stereotyped replies, constantly at a loss when faced with the truth, from which it nevertheless claimed to derive its laws. The left is schizophrenic and needs doctoring through pitiless self criticism, exercise of the heart, close reasoning, and a little modesty. [3]

---

1. Lev Braun. *Witness to Decline, Albert Camus: Moralist of the Absurd*. Rutherford: Fairleigh Dickinson University Press, 1974, p.241.

2. Ibid.

3. Albert Camus. *Resistance, Rebellion, and Death*. New York: Alfred A. Knopf, 1961, p. 171.

This passage demonstrates that Camus was in fact the true revolutionary. All genuinely constructive reflection clears the way for true and lasting peace by voicing a sincere, apolitical opposition to all forms of totalitarianism. Camus' trajectories as man and thinker were conjoined in a life that was dedicated to the search for truth. His individualism, dignity and personal autonomy brought him a great deal of strife and personal antagonism from people who had something to gain from denying him these basic human qualities. This antagonism and hate that he underwent were partly due to the mechanism and, if we are to call things by their proper name, the technique of terror that ideologues had so eagerly perfected already in the early part of the twentieth century. Camus, like so many other writers (Stanislaw Witkiewicz, Alexander Solzhenitsyn, Nadezhda Mandelstam and Boris Pasternak, to name just a few) valued human integrity and autonomy and he was a victim of a ruthless worldview that denies any inherent value to the individual.[1]

Like Heidegger, who thought that only a God could save modern man, Camus too, if we are to judge by *The First Man*, grew more restless and less optimistic when he realized that the absurd had become institutionalized in the form of the totalitarian state. His concern had always been for what Unamuno (in *The Tragic Sense of Life*) called the individual man of flesh and bones. The individual, Camus argued, ought to be the main concern of all genuine humanism and not an abstract ideological rendition of man.[2]

---

1. See the works of Witkiewicz, Solzhenitsyn and Mandelstam.

2. Miguel de Unamuno. *Del Sentimiento Tragico de la Vida*. Madrid: Editorial Plenitud, 1966, p. 7.

WORKS CITED

Alain. *The Gods*. Translated from the French by Richard Pevear. London: Quartet Encounters, 1988.

Ambler, Eric. *The Schirmer Inheritance*. New York. Alfred A. Knopf, 1953.

_____. Waiting For Orders: The Complete Short Stories of Eric Ambler. New York: The Mysterious Press, 1991.

_____. *Here Lies Eric Ambler: An Autobiography*. Glasgow: Fontana/Collins, 1986.

_____. *Epitaph for A Spy*. New York: Bantam Books, 1965.

_____. *Journey Into Fear*. New York: Ballantine Books, 1977.

_____. *A Coffin for Dimitrios*. Cleveland: The World Publishing Company, 1939.

_____. *Doctor Frigo*. New York: Atheneum, 1974.

_____. The Siege of the Villa Lipp. New York: Random House, 1977.

_____. *The Care of Time*. New York: Farrar Straus Giroux, 1981.

_____. *The Light of Day*. New York: Ballantine Books, 1962.

_____. *To Catch A Spy: An Anthology of Favorite Spy Stories*. Ed. Eric Ambler. New York: Bantam Books, 1966.

_____. *Cause For Alarm*. New York: Bantam Books, 1974.

_____. *Judgment on Deltchev*. New York: Carroll and Graf Publishers, Inc., 1991.

_____. *The Levanter*. New York: Bantam Books, 1972.

_____. *Background to Danger*. New York: Bantam, 1968. Ambrosetti, Ronald J. *Eric Ambler*. New York: Twayne Publishers, 1994.

Amis, Kingsley. *The James Bond Dossier: Is He in Hell or is He in Heaven – that Damned Elusive 007?* New York: The New American Library, 1965.

Arnheim, Rudolf. *Film as Art*. Berkeley: University of California, 1971.

Arendt, Hannah. *Eight Exercises in Political Thought: Between Past and Future*. New York: Penguin Books, 1980.

Assis, Machado de. *Epitaph of A Small Winner*. Translated from the Portuguese by William L. Grossman. New York: Avon Books, 1978.

Atkins, John. *The British Spy Novel: Styles in Treachery*. London: John Calder Press, 1984.

Barrett, William. *Time of Need: Forms of Imagination in the Twentieth Century*. New York: Harper & Row Publishers, 1972.

_____. *The Illusion of Technique. A Search for Meaning in a Technological Civilization*. Garden City: Anchor Books, 1979.

_____. *The Death of the Soul: From Descartes to the Computer*. New York: Doubleday, 1986.

Barzun, Jacques and Wendell Hertig Taylor. Ed. *A Catalogue of Crime: Being a Reader's Guide to Literature of Mystery, Detection, and Related Genres*. New York: Harper and Row, Publishers, 1971.

Baudelaire, Charles. *Paris Spleen*. Translated from the French by Louse Varese. New York: New Directions Book, 1970.

Bencivenga, Ermanno. *Logic and Other Nonsense: The Case of Anselm and His God*. Princeton, New Jersey: Princeton University Press, 1993.

Bergier, Jacques and Pauwels, Louis. *El Retorno de los Brujos*. Barcelona: Plaza & Janes, 1981.

Berlin, Isaiah. *Essays In The History of Ideas*. New York: The Viking Press, 1955.

Bloom, Harold. *Omens of Millennium: The Gnosis of Angels, Dreams, and Resurrection*. New York: Riverhead Head Books, 1996.

Boggs, Joseph M. *The Art of Watching Films*. Mountain View: Mayfield Publishing, 1991.

Boorstin, Daniel J. *The Creators: A History of Heroes of the Imagination*. New York: Random House, 1992. Borges, Jorge Luis. *Textos Cautivos*. Madrid: Alianza Editorial, 1998.

_____. *Selected Non-Fiction*. Ed. By Eliot Weinberger. New York: Penguin Books, 1999.

Bradley, G. David. *A Guide to the World's Religions*. Englewood Cliffs, N.J: Prentice-Hall, Inc., 1963.

Brandon, Ruth. *Surreal Lives, The surrealists: 1917-1945*. New York: Grove Press, 1999.

Braun, Lev. *Witness to Decline, Albert Camus: Moralist of the Absurd*. Rutherford: Fairleigh Dickinson University Press, 1974.

Bree, Germaine. *Camus*. New Brunswick: Rutgers University Press, 1964.
_____. *Camus and Sartre: Crisis and Commitment*. New York: A Delta Book, 1972. Breton, Andre. *Manifestoes of Surrealism*. Ann Arbor: The University of Michigan Press, 1972.

Brown, Frederick. *An Impersonation of Angels: A Biography of Jean Cocteau*. New York: The Viking Press, 1968.

Burke, Frank. *Federico Fellini: Variety Lights to La Dolce Vita*. Boston: Twayne Publishers, 1984.

Calderón de la Barca, Pedro. *Life Is a Dream*. New York: Hill & Wang, 1970.

Copleston, Frederick S.J. *History Of Philosophy*. New York: Image Books, 1963.

Camus, Albert. *The Myth of Sisyphus and Other Essays*. (New York: Vintage International, 1983), p.63.

_____. *The Rebel: An Essay on Man in Revolt*. Translated by Anthony Bower. New York: Vintage International, 1991.

_____. *The First Man*. Translated by David Hapgood. New York: Vintage International, 1996.

_____. *Resistance, Rebellion, and Death*. Translated by Justin O'Brien. New York: Alfred A. Knopf, 1961.

_____. *A Happy Death*. Translated by Richard Howard. New York: Alfred A. Knopf, 1972.

_____. *The Plague*. Translated by Stuart Gilbert. New York: Vintage Books, 1972.

_____. *Exile and the Kingdom*. Translated by Justin O'Brien. New York: Vintage International, 1991.

_____. *Notebooks: 1935-1942*. Translated by Philip Thody. New York: Alfred A. Knopf, 1963.

Canetti, Elías. *Auto-Da-Fe*. Translated by C.V. Wedgwood. New York: Farrar Straus Giroux, 1974.

Cassirer, Ernst. An *Essay on Man: An Introduction to a Philosophy of Human Culture*. New Haven: Yale University Press, 1972.

_____. *Rousseau, Kant and Goethe*. New York: Harper Torchbooks, 1963.

Cavell, Stanley. The World Viewed: Reflection on the Ontology of Film. Cambridge: Harvard University Press, 1979.

_____. *Philosophical Passages: Wittgenstein, Emerson, Austin, Derrida*. Oxford: Basil Blackwell, Ltd. 1995.

Celine, Louis-Ferdinand. *Castle to Castle*. Translated by Ralph Manheim. New York: Delacorte Press, 1968.

_____. *Death on the Installment Plan*. Translated by Ralph Manheim. New York: A New Directions Book, 1966.

_____. *London Bridge: Guignol's Band II*. Translated by Dominic Di Bernardi. New York: Dalkey Archive Press, 1955.

_____. *Journey to the End of the Night*. Translated by H. P. Marks. New York: A New Directions Book, 1960.

_____. *Rigadoon*. Translated by Ralph Manheim. New York: Delacorte Press, 1974. Cicero, Marcus Tullius. *Selected Letters*. London: Penguin Books, 1986.

Charon, Jean. *Cosmology: Theories of the Universe*. New York: McGraw-Hill Book Company. 1970.

Chesterton, G.K. *The Man Who Was Thursday*. New York: Dover Publications, Inc., 1986. _____. *The Paradoxes of Mr. Pond*. New York: Dover Publications, Inc., 1990.

_____. *The Father Brown Omnibus*. New York: Dodd, Mead and Company, 1951.

_____. *The Common Man*. New York: Sheed and Ward, 1950.

_____. *What's Wrong with the World?* Peru, Illinois: Sherwood, Sugder & Company.

Cioran. E.M. *The New Gods*. Translated by Richard Howard. New York: Quadrangle, 1974.

Clifton, Roy N. *The Figure in Film*. East Brunswick: Associated University Press, 1983.

Confucius. *Confucian Analects, The Great Learning & The Doctrine of the Man*. Translated by James Legge. New York: Dover Publication, Inc., 1971.

Crispin, Edmund. *The Moving Toyshop*. New York: Penguin Books, 1979.

Cocteau, Jean. *Diary of an Unknown*. Translated by Jesse Browner. New York: Paragon House, 1991.

_____. *Art and Faith: Letters between Jacques Maritain and Jean Cocteau*. New York: Philosophical Library, 1948.

_____. *Professional Secrets: An Autobiography of Jean Cocteau*. Translated from the French by Richard Howard. New York: Farrar, Straus and Giroux, Inc., 1970.

_____. *My Contemporaries*. New York: Chilton Book Company, 1968.

_____. *Past Tense: The Complete Cocteau Diaries, Volume Two*. San Diego: Harcourt Brace Jovanovich, Publishers, 1988.

Croce, Benedetto. *Lógica Como Ciencia del Concepto Puro: Lógica Conceptual y su Implicación en la Historia de la Filosofia*. México: Ediciones Contraste, 1980. Defoe, Daniel. *Robinson Crusoe: Travels and Adventures*. The Spencer Press, 1937.

Dennett, Daniel. *Kinds of Minds: Toward an Understanding of Consciousness*. New York: BasicBooks, 1996.

Dewey, John. *Reconstruction in Philosophy*. New York: Mentor Books, 1951.

Dick, Philip K. *The Shifting Realities of Philip K. Dick: Selected Literary and Philosophical Writings*. Ed. By Lawrence Sutin. New York: Pantheon Books, 1995.

Doren, Van Charles. *A History of Knowledge: The Pivotal Events, People, and Achievements of World History*. New York: Ballantine Books, 1991.

Dostoyevsky, Fyodor. *Notes From Underground*. Translated by Andrew R. MacAndrew. New York: Signet Classic, 1980. Doyle, Arthur Conan. *The Edge of the Unknown*. New York: Barnes and Noble, 1992.

Dunham, Lowell and Ivar Ivask. Ed. *The Cardinal Points of Borges*. Norman: University of Oklahoma Press, 1971.

Edwards, Paul. *Encyclopedia of Philosophy*. Editor. New York: Macmillan Publishing Co., Inc. & The Free Press, 1967.

Erasmus. *Ten Colloquies*. Translated by Craig R. Thompson. New York: Bobbs-Merrill Educational Publishing, 1957.

Ferry, Luc. *Man Made God: The Meaning of Life.* Translated from the French by David Pellauer. Chicago: The University of Chicago Press, 2002.

Flew, Anthony. *God, Freedom and Immortality: A Critical Analysis.* New York: Prometheus Books, 1984.

Frazer, James G. *The Golden Bough: The Roots of Religion and Folklore.* New York: Gramercy Books, 1981.

Fukuyama, Francis. *The End of History and the Last Man.* New York: The Free Press, 1992.

Gary, Romain. *Your Ticket is No Longer Valid.* Translated by Sophie Wilkens. New York: George Braziller, 1977.

Geduld, Harry M. Editor. *Authors on Film.* Bloomington: Indiana University Press, 1972. *The Epic of Gilgamesh.* Translated by N.K. Sandars. London: Penguin Books, 1972.

Gide, Andre. *The Immoralist.* Translated by Richard Howard. New York: Alfred A. Knopf, 1970. Gilson Etienne. *God and Philosophy.* New Haven: Yale University Press, 1969.

Gironella, José Maria. *Los fantasmas de mi cerebro.* Barcelona: Editorial Planeta, 1972.

Gracian, Baltasar. *The Art of Worldly Wisdom.* Translated by Christopher Maurer. New York: Doubleday, 1992.

Grimsley, Ronald. *Existentialist Thought.* Cardiff: University of Wales Press, 1967. Grene, David and Richmond Lattimore. Editors. *Sophocles II: The Complete Greek Tragedies.* Chicago: The University of Chicago Press, 1969.

Hamilton, Edith. *The Greek Way.* New York: W. W. Norton & Company, Inc., 1930.

Harman, Mark. *Robert Walser Rediscovered: Stories, Fairy-Tale Plays, and Critical Responses.* Editor. Hanover: University Press of New England, 1985.

Haycraft, Howard. *The Art of The Mystery Story: A Collection of Critical Essays.* New York: Simon and Schuster, 1946.

_____. *Murder for Pleasure: The Life and Times of the Detective Story.* New York: Appleton, 1941.

Hillier, Jim. Editor. *Cahiers du Cinema: The 1950s, New-Realism, Hollywood, New Wave.* Cambridge: Harvard University Press, 1985.

Horgan, John. *The Undiscovered Mind: How the Human Brain Defies Replication, Medication, and Explanation.* New York: The Free Press, 1999.

Hubben, William. *Dostoevsky, Kierkegaard, Nietzsche, and Kafka*. New York: Collier Books, 1962.

Infante, Guillermo Cabrera. *Arcadia Todas Las Noches*. Bogota: Editorial La Oveja Negra, Ltda., 1987.

_____. *Un Oficio Del Siglo XX*. Bogota: Editorial Oveja Negra, 1987.

Ingenieros, José. *Las Fuerza Morales*. Buenos Aires: Editorial Losada, 1968.

Issari, Ali M. *Cinema Verite*. Kalamazoo: Michigan State University Press, 1971.

James, William. *The Varieties of Religious Experience: A Sturdy in Human Nature*. Introduction by Reinhold Niebuhr. New York: Collier Books, 1961.

Jaspers, Karl. *Philosophy of Existence*. Translated by Richard F. Grabau. College Station: University of Pennsylvania Press, 1971.

_____. *Way To Wisdom: An Introduction*. Translated by Ralph Manheim. New Haven & London: Yale University Press, 1954.

Jullian, Philippe. *Dreamers of Decadence*. New York: Praeger Publishers, 1971.

Kaufmann, Walter. *Tragedy and Philosophy*. New York: Anchor Books, 1968.

_____. *Existentialism from Dostoevsky to Sartre*. New York. New American Library, 1975.

Kellett, E.E. *A Short History of Religions*. Baltimore: Penguin Books, 1962.

Klosko, George. *The Development of Plato's Political Theory*. New York: Methuen, 1986.

Koestler, Arthur. *Darkness at Noon*. Translated by Daphne Hardy. New York: Bantam Books, 1972.

Kolakowski, Leszek. *Religion*. New York: Fontana Press, 1983.

_____. *Modernity on Endless Trial*. Chicago: The University of Chicago Press, 1990.

Kramer, Victor A. and Lawson, Lewis A. *Conversations With Walker Percy*. Jackson: University of Mississippi Press, 1985.

La Rochefoucauld. *Maxims*. Translated by Leonard Tancock. New York: Penguin Books, 1959.

Larkin, Philip. *Required Writing: Miscellaneous Pieces 1955-1982*. London: Faber and Faber, 1983.

Lehman, David. *The Last Avant-Garde: The Making of the New York School of Poets*. New York: Doubleday, 1998.

Leroux, Jeannine Verdes. *Deconstructing Pierre Bourdieu: Against Sociological Terrorism from the Left*. New York: Algora Publishing, 2001.

Levi-Strauss, Claude. *Structural Anthropology*. New York: Basic Books, Inc., 1963.

Lewis, C.S. *The Abolition of Man: How Education Develops Man's Sense of Morality*. New York: Macmillan Publishing Co., Inc., 1978.

Lewis, Wyndham. *Rude Assignment: An Intellectual Autobiography*. Santa Barbara: Black Sparrow Press, 1984.

Lehman, David. *The Last Avant-Garde: The Making of the New York School of Poets*. New York: Doubleday, 1998.

Lonergan, Martin J. "Gabriel Marcel's Philosophy of Death." *Philosophy Today*. Spring 1975.

Lottman, Herbert R. *Albert Camus*. New York: Doubleday & Company, Inc., 1979.

Lurker, Manfred. *The Gods and Symbols of Ancient Egypt*. London: Thames and Hudson, 1974.

Madariaga de, Salvador. *Portrait of a Man Standing*. University: University of Alabama Press, 1968.

Mandelstam, Nadezhda. *Hope Against Hope*. Translated from the Russian by Max Hayward. New York: Atheneum, 1983.

Marias, Javier. *When I Was Mortal*. Translated by Margaret Jull Costa. New York: New Directions Books, 1996.

Marias, Julián. *El Cine: Volumen I, Escritos Sobre Cine (1960-1965)*. Madrid: Royal Books, 1994.

_____. Metaphysical Anthropology: The Empirical Structure of Human Life. Translated by Frances M. Lopez-Morillas. University Park: Pennsylvania State University Press, 1971.

_____. *Jose Ortega y Gasset: Circumstance and Vocation*. Translated by Frances M. Lopez Morillas. Norman: University of Oklahoma Press, 1970.

_____. *America in the Fifties and Sixties: Julian Marias On the United States*. Translated by Blanche De Puy and Harold C. Raley. University Park: The Pennsylvania State University Press, 1972.

_____. *Filosofia Española Actual: Unamuno, Ortega, Morente, Zubiri*. Madrid: Colección Austral, Espasa-Calpe, S.A.

_____. *Philosophy as Dramatic Theory*. Translated by James Parsons. University Park: The Pennsylvania State University Press, 1971.

Masterson, Patrick. *Atheism and Alienation: A Study of the Philosophical Sources of Contemporary Atheism.* Middlesex, England: Penguin Books, 1973.

Maugham, Somerset W. *The Summing Up.* New York: The Literary Guild of America, Inc., 1938.

_____. *Ashenden: The British Agent.* New York: Avon Books, 1951.

_____. *Selected Prefaces and Introductions of W. Somerset Maugham.* Garden City: Doubleday & Company, Inc., 1963.

Maximov, Vladimir. *A Man Survives.* Translated by Anselm Hollo. New York: Grove Press, In., 1962.

McGuire, Jeremiah C. *Cinema and Value Philosophy.* New York: Philosophical Library, 1968.

McCarthy, Patrick. *Camus.* New York: Random House, 1982.

Milosz, Czeslaw. *The Captive Mind.* Translated by Jane Zielonko. New York: Vintage International, 1981.

_____. *To Begin Where I Am: Selected Essays.* Edited by Bogdana Carpenter and Madeline G. Levine. New York: Farrar, Straus and Giroux, 2001.

Motion, Andrew. *Philip Larkin: A Writer's Life.* New York: Farrar, Straus and Giroux, 1993.

Muggeridge, Malcolm. *A Third Testament.* New York: Ballantine Books, 1983.

Nietzsche, Friedrich. *Beyond Good And Evil: Prelude to a Philosophy of the Future.* Translated with commentary by Walter Kaufmann. New York: Vintage Press, 1966.

Nigosian, S.A.: *The Zoroastrian Faith Tradition & Modern Research.* Montreal: McGill-Queen University Press, 1993.

O'Brien, Conor Cruise. *Albert Camus of Europe and Africa.* New York: The Viking Press, 1970.

Oesterreich, T.K. *Possession: Demoniacal & Other.* Secaucus, New Jersey: The Citadel Press, 1964.

Ortega y Gasset, José. *Meditations on Hunting.* New York: Charles Scribner's Sons, 1985.

_____. *The Revolt of the Masses.* New York: W.W. Norton & Company, 1993.

_____. *Espana Invertebrada.* Madrid: Revista de Occidente, 1971.

_____. *The Modern Theme.* Translated by James Cleugh. New Cork: Harper Torchbooks, 1961.

Owens, Joseph. *A History of Ancient Western Philosophy*. New York: Appleton, Century, Crofts, Inc., 1959.

Pauwels, Louis and Jacques Bergier. *El retorno de los brujos*. Madrid: Plaza & James, 1981.

Pearce, Joseph Chilton. *The Crack in the Cosmic Egg: Challenging Constructs of Mind and Reality*. New York: A Quokka Book, 1971.

Percy, Walker. *Lancelot*. New York: Farrar, Straus and Giroux, 1977. p. 3. Pohl, Frederik. *The Way The Future Was*. London: Victor Gollancz, Ltd., 1979.

Polanyi, Michael. *The Logic of Liberty: Reflections and Rejoiners*. Indianapolis: Liberty Fund, 1998.

Piñera, Virgilio. *Cold Tales*. New York: Eridanus Press, 1988.

Proust, Marcel. *On Art and Literature: 1896-1919*. Translated by Slyvia Townsend Warner. New York: Carroll and Graf Publishers, Inc., 1997.

Putnam, Hilary. *The Many Faces of Realism*. LaSalle, Illinois: Open Court, 1991.

Renaut, Alain. *The Era of the Individual: A Contribution to a History of Subjectivity*. Translated by M.B. DeBevoise and Franklin Philip. Princeton: Princeton University Press, 1999.

Revel, Jean-Francois. *Anti-Americanism*. Translated by Diarmid Cammell. San Francisco: Encounter Books, 2003.

Reynolds, Barbara. *Dorothy L. Sayers: Her Life and Soul*. New York: St. Martin's Press, 1993.

Santayana, George. *The Philosophy of Santayana*. Edited by Irwin Edman. New York: Charles Scribner's Son, 1936.

Sartre, Jean-Paul. *Situations*. Translated from the French by Benita Eisler. Greenwich Conn.: Fawcett Crest Book, 1965.

Savater, Fernando. *Mira Por Donde: Autobiografía Razonada*. Madrid: Taurus, 2003.

Scruton, Roger. *An Intelligent Person's Guide to Modern Culture*. London: Duckworth Publishers, 1998.

Searle, John R. *The Rediscovery of Mind*. Cambridge, Massachusetts: The MIT Press, 1992.

Shakespeare, William. *The Complete Works: Hamlet*, I, V, 165. Alfred Harbage, General Editor. New York: The Viking Press, 1986.

Simon, John. *Movies Into Film: Film Criticism 1967-1970*. New York: The Dial Press, 1971.

Symons, Julian. *The Telltale Heart: The Life and Work of Edgar Allan Poe.* New York: Harper and Row, Publishers, 1978.

Svevo, Italo. *Confessions of Zeno.* Translated from the Italian by Beryl De Zoete. New York: Vintage Books, 1958. p.3.

Taffel, David. *Nietzsche Unbound: The Struggle for Spirit in the Age of Science.* St. Paul: Paragon House, 2003

Templeton, Kenneth, Jr. Editor. *The Politicization of Society.* Indianapolis: Liberty Fund, 1979.

Thody, Philip. *Albert Camus: A Study of his Work.* New York: Grove Press, Inc., 1959.

Todd, Olivier. *Albert Camus: A Life.* Translated by Benjamin Ivry. New York: Alfred A. Knopf, 1999.

Tyler, Parker. *Early Classics of the Foreign Film.* New York: A Citadel Press Book, 1962. Unamuno, Miguel de. *Niebla.* Madrid: Taurus Ediciones, 1967.

_____. *Del Sentimiento Trágico de la Vida En Los Hombres y En Los Pueblos.* Madrid, Espana: Editorial Plenitud, 1966.

Vitoux, Frederic. *Celine: A Biography.* Translated by Jesse Browner. New York: Paragon House, 1992.

Yeats, William Butler. *Eleven Plays.* Edited by A. Norman Jeffares. New York: Collier Books, 1964.

Walser, Robert. *Masquerade and Other Stories.* Translated by Susan Bernofsky. Baltimore: The Johns Hopkins University Press, 1990.

Weiss, Paul. *Cinematics.* Carbondale: Southern Illinois University Press, 1975 Whitehead, Alfred North. *Modes of Thoughts.* New York: The Free Press, 1968.

Wilson, Colin. *Beyond the Outsider.* New York: Carroll & Graff Publishers Inc., 1965.

_____. *Religion and the Rebel*: Bath: Ashgrove Press, 1992.

Wollen, Peter. *Sign and Meaning in the Cinema.* Bloomington: Indiana University Press, 1969.

Witkiewicz, Stanislaw Ignacy. *The Witkiewicz Reader.* Translated by Daniel Gerould. (Evanston: Northwestern University Press, 1992) p. 285.

_____. *Insatiability.* Translated by Louis Iribarne. Evanston: Northwestern University Press, 1996.

_____. *The Mother & Other Unsavory Plays*. Translated by Daniel Gerould. New York: Applause, 1993.

_____. *The Madman and the Nun and The Crazy Locomotive*. Translated by Daniel Gerould.

Zola, Emile. *The Works of Emile Zola*. Roslyn, New York: Blacks Readers Service Company, 1928.

INDEX